KU-629-877

# Spirit TALK

## Hearing the Voice of God

# LARRY RANDOLPH

## MorningStar Publications
A DIVISION OF MORNINGSTAR FELLOWSHIP CHURCH
375 Star Light Drive, Fort Mill, SC 29715

*Spirit Talk*
Copyright © 2005 by Larry Randolph
Third Printing, 2007

Distributed by MorningStar Publications, Inc., a division of MorningStar
Fellowship Church, 375 Star Light Drive, Fort Mill, SC 29715

International Standard Book Number: 1-929371-51-9; 978-1-929371-51-8

MorningStar's website: www.morningstarministries.org
For information call 1-800-542-0278.

Larry Randolph Ministries
P.O. Box 157, Moravian Falls, NC 28654-0157
Website: www.larryrandolph.com / E-mail: Info@larryrandolph.com
For information call: (336) 921-4447

Cover design and book layout by Dana Zondory

Unless otherwise indicated, all Scripture quotations are taken from the New
American Standard Bible, copyright © 1960, 1962, 1963, 1968, 1971, 1973, 1974,
1977 by The Lockman Foundation. Italics in Scripture are for emphasis only.

No part of this book may be reproduced or transmitted in any form or by any
means, electronic, mechanical, including photocopying, recording, or by any
information storage and retrieval system, without written permission from
the author.

All rights reserved.
Printed in the United States of America.

# Contents

# Dedication

This book is dedicated to my Lord who often talks to me in strange and unusual ways. I am so grateful that You take time to communicate with me, even when I don't understand and when I am just not listening. Please don't stop talking! I love the sound of Your voice no matter what shape or form it takes. You are indeed an awesome God and I love You totally and unconditionally. You have my eternal attention.

Also, my deepest affection goes to my wife, Laura, who continually encourages me to be the man I am called to be. Your beautiful spirit and passion for intimacy with God serves as a priceless model of Christian character in my life. Because of your continual support and encouragement, I have found the courage to go forward in life. You are my spirit-mate, my soul-mate, and the woman of my dreams. I love you completely.

# Introduction

*T*HE WORLD IS FAST APPROACHING AN ERA OF supernatural awareness. Fortune-telling, telepathic communication, palmistry, horoscope predictions, and other paranormal activities are experiencing a revival of popularity in this nation. Our desire to hear from the other side has spawned a host of psychics for hire and other mediums of celebrity status that reportedly see our past, predict our future, and communicate with our dead relatives. On a daily basis, we are bombarded with the sound of psychic chatter promising insight into the unknown.

What does all this tell us? People want to hear from a source greater than themselves and often settle for imitations. Not realizing that God clearly speaks today, many seekers chase shadows instead of the real thing. Even so, this pursuit is not always hopeless because a shadow is nothing more than a distortion of a real object. And, the bigger and more defined the shadow becomes, the closer we are to the real thing.

The same is true of the shadow cast by pseudo-spiritualism. It is a distorted reflection of that which is real, and the presence of this shadow serves as a sign that true spiritual phenomena exists. In fact, many people today have abandoned their pursuit of counterfeit spiritualism and are now experiencing unprecedented encounters with the Spirit of God through signs and wonders, dreams, visions, divine appearances, and other extraordinary manifestations.

Regardless that this phenomena is a by-product of the Christian experience, history tells us when believers embrace new levels of spiritual phenomena, we confuse the shadow with the substance. Every time we make the transition from one realm of glory to another, the line that separates divination from the divine is often blurred by our inability to discern between the true and the counterfeit. The past result has been spiritual chaos in the church.

What then is the answer to this problem? Should we neglect our moment of visitation because of our past failures? Do we relegate ownership of the spiritual world to the unsaved? Or, do we look beyond our poor track record and embrace fresh levels of the supernatural?

Although we run the risk of opening a Pandora's box of confusion, I believe it is necessary for the body of Christ to break out of our mental prison of regret. Regardless of our reputation for mixture, we must not hold back in fear or entertain the possibility of deception. The apostle Paul, for instance, encouraged the expression of spiritual gifts in the Corinthian church, knowing that these things would be misinterpreted, counterfeited, and abused. His decision to lead the people of God into the supernatural was based on trust in the Holy Spirit's ability to bring them to maturity, not on the merits of their character or worthiness.

In view of this, I named this book, *Spirit Talk*. Regardless of our predisposition to immaturity, I am convinced that God has opened the gates of heaven and is speaking to us in diverse and extraordinary ways. Although many will abuse this privilege and mix the real with the counterfeit, the Holy Spirit will eventually sort out the precious from the vile.

With these things in mind, I have attempted to chronicle several methods of communication which are both personally familiar to me and biblically relevant. In no way does the following information remotely cover the inexhaustible subject of hearing from heaven, nor do I believe that it will pacify the inquisitive nature of the theological mind. It is simply an attempt to address the phenomenon of Spirit talk by communicating personal stories and offering practical wisdom that can help believers in the quest to hear from heaven.

Finally, I have been told that this subject would be better served if I referred to the spiritual encounters of others instead of firsthand experiences. Certainly, there are people who have a richer history in this area than I have—some of them being my closest friends. However, I do not feel that I can write authoritatively about this subject by relating someone else's journey into the

Spirit realm. To keep it simple and honest, I have drawn from my own well of experience as accurately as I can remember. Perhaps this will give hope to those who are reluctant to acknowledge that God could be speaking to them in strange and unusual ways.

*Larry Randolph*

CHAPTER ONE

# Spiritual Ears and Eyes

**They heard the sound of the LORD God walking in the garden in the cool of the day...**

**Then the Lord God called to the man and said to him, "Where are you?"(Genesis 3:8-9).**

SAINT JOHN DECLARED IN REVELATION 2:11 **"HE who has an ear, let him hear what the Spirit says to the churches..."**

As a young man, I often wondered what John really meant by those words. Is God really a talking God? If so, can we develop an ear to hear from heaven?

The answer to both questions is an emphatic YES! Apparently, God is a prolific communicator and emphasized His desire to speak and be heard when He declared more than one thousand times in Scripture, **"Thus says the Lord."** What's more, the book of Revelation depicts the heavenly realm as a noisy place where tons of information is constantly being processed and conveyed to earth.

In regard to the question of hearing from God, the Bible is filled with testimonies of men and women who heard the sound of His voice. This phenomenon was evident in the beginning of the Bible when Adam heard the sound of God's voice in the cool of the day and is also found in numerous chapters of the Bible thereafter.

In Matthew 17:5, for example, three disciples on the Mount of Transfiguration heard a voice from heaven announcing the deity of Jesus. In Revelation 1:10, John the revelator also recognized the voice of the resurrected Christ speaking as a trumpet and fell at His feet in reverent awe. John's response to the heavenly voice was a testimony to the Lord's earlier declaration in John 10:4-5 that His sheep would follow Him primarily because they were able to distinguish His voice from others.

## The Sound of His Voice

The problem with hearing from heaven is that God does not exist as a human being. He is a multi-dimensional spiritual entity who communicates in thousands of different ways and on many different spiritual frequencies. He does not think like a human, act like a human, or talk like a human. His primary language is not English, Spanish, German, French, or any other earthly dialect.

It is true that God converses with us on a human level, but His communication skills are light-years beyond the realm of human speech. He can convey in a millisecond more information than we can enunciate in a thousand generations. Any attempt, therefore, to confine God to the box of human language would be like cramming the universe into the nucleus of an atom.

The bottom line is that the sound of God's voice entails much more than the noise made and heard by the verbalization of a particular language. Genesis 3:8 states that Adam **"heard the voice of the Lord God walking in the garden in the cool of the day" (KJV),** which supports this truth when you consider that the word **"voice"** is translated from the Hebrew word *kole* meaning sound, and the word **"cool"** is translated from the Hebrew word *ruach* meaning wind. The implication is that Adam heard daily the sound of God's presence stirring in the wind. A similar phenomenon is also found in Acts 2:2 when God communicated His heart on the day of Pentecost with a sound from heaven like a mighty rushing wind.

God's communication skills are light-years beyond the realm of human speech.

God also spoke to our spiritual forefathers by means and methods unfamiliar to most Christians today. Moses encountered the Lord in a fiery bush, and later heard His voice through thunder and lightning on Mount Sinai (see Exodus 3 and Exodus 19). Prophets Elijah and Elisha saw the Almighty in a flaming chariot (see II Kings 2); whereas, King David heard the Spirit of God moving in the tops of the mulberry trees (see II Samuel 5:24-25). In the last book of the Bible, John heard the voice of the Lord as the sound of many waters (see Revelation 1:15).

The Apostle Paul confirmed the diversity of spiritual communication when he wrote in Romans 1:20 that the invisible things of God are made known to us by the things which He has created. In other words, God is speaking through His handiwork. This includes the earth, stars, planets, animal kingdom, plant kingdom, and other aspects of nature. On a rare occasion in Numbers 22:28, the Almighty also spoke through a donkey, confirming once again that His language is extraordinarily diverse.

## Multidimensional Hearing

To complicate matters, humans made in the image of God are also uniquely diverse. No two people are exactly the same. We all have the same basic design, but under no circumstances do we feel, reason, act, think, or communicate in exactly the same way. The manner in which we hear from God varies according to the uniqueness of our personality, our emotional and spiritual make-up, and other distinct characteristics. Perhaps this is the reason a number of people in John 12:29 heard the majestic voice of God at Jesus' baptism, while others said it only thundered.

That which is Spirit talk to some is no doubt indiscriminate noise to others. This is again due to the immense diversity which exists in the realm of human awareness and perception. The problem also lies in our reluctance to break out of our familiar mode of hearing. In the same way that we have limited God's voice to the realm of human dialect, we have also limited our receiving from God to the hearing of the ear. Consequently, we live in a one-dimensional realm of communication.

In light of this limitation, it is a relief to know that God's voice is not limited to words, nor is our hearing limited to the function of the ear. Actually, all of creation is a credible voice, and the human body is like a giant ear that processes thousands of pieces of information from every spectrum of life. Furthermore, the mind, soul, and spirit of man are basically molded by information received through our physical senses. What the ear and the eye take in, the human mind processes and communicates to the spirit of man. The same is true of taste, smell, and touch. They, too, are information conductors that pass on data to our conscious and subconscious mind.

> The human body is like a giant ear that processes thousands of pieces of information from every spectrum of life.

Categorically speaking, believers are privileged to hear God through the five physical senses. He also communicates to us through inner voice, inspired thought, impressions, dreams, visions, trances, and other methods of Spirit talk that will be addressed in the following chapters.

Bear in mind, however, that manifestations which are not influenced *by* or do not bear witness *to* the person of the Holy Spirit needs to be discarded. This is essential if you consider that the voice of the Holy Spirit is the collective voice of the Godhead (see John 14:26) and His job is to bridge the communication gap between heaven and earth. Paul declared in I Corinthians 2:10-13 that the heart of God is revealed to us by the Holy Spirit **"...so that we may know the things freely given to us by God."**

**The Mystery of Sight and Sound**

To better understand the complex nature of spiritual communication, one has only to look at the mystery of sight and sound. The role these two dynamics play in the natural realm provides us with a vast amount of information that can be applied to the subject of Spirit talk.

To illustrate, sound is a physical phenomenon which stimulates the sense of hearing. This hearing begins with sound waves made from the vibrations and movement of physical objects—such as the vibrating strings of a violin, the vibrations made by the wings of an insect, or the sound that resonates from vibrations made by air passing out of human lungs and over the vocal cords. These sound waves travel through the atmosphere and enter a normal human ear causing changes in the air pressure of the outer ear canal. The waves are then amplified and transmitted by the eardrum causing vibrations that are detected by nerve fibers in the inner ear. These signals are transmitted by the auditory nerve to the brain where information is processed, interpreted, and distributed to the appropriate areas of the human conscience.

The phenomenon of natural vision is somewhat the same. Vision begins with light rays bouncing off the surface of objects around us. These reflected rays travel through the atmosphere and enter the eyeball where they are assimilated and focused. The final destination is a layer of nerve tissue at the back of the eye where the light is transformed into electrical signals that travel through the optic nerve to the visual area of the brain. Brain cells then decode the signals into images, providing us with sight.

Why the lesson on sight and sound? As natural vision is the result of reflected light from physical objects, spiritual vision comes from the reflected light of God in the spirit world. Also, in the same way that physical sound is the result of vibrations carried through the atmosphere by sound waves, supernatural hearing comes from heavenly vibrations transmitted by spiritual sound waves in the spirit realm.

Now the important questions: Does the fact that blind people cannot see reflected light rays mean there is nothing in front of them? Does the fact that deaf people are unable to perceive and interpret sound waves mean that nothing is being said to them?

The obvious answer to both questions is "no." More importantly, this principle applies to the realm of spiritual communication. The fact that we do not hear or see the spirit world does not indicate the absence of God's voice any more than the blindness or deafness of a person invalidates the existence of the physical world around them. The truth is that God constantly broadcasts information on every wavelength and frequency known to creation.

## Broken Receivers

I am convinced the problem of poor communication is not with God, but with the fact that we have either lost our signal from heaven or that our spiritual receiver is broken. This should come as no surprise if we understand that our spiritual eyes and ears are impaired as a result of the fallen state of mankind. When Adam and Eve fell from their estate in the Garden of Eden, spiritual darkness invaded their eyes and ears and was passed from generation to generation.

What is the answer to this dilemma? How does mankind re-connect with the spirit realm?

We must understand that the primary source of true spiritual light comes from the blessed Trinity. In James 1:17, God is called the **"Father of lights,"** and in John 8:12, Christ declared Himself to be the **"Light of the world."** Saint John also declared that Jesus is the word and expression of God that came to earth and gave His life so humanity could connect to heaven. Therefore, to gain legal access into the spirit world, we must embrace the door to that realm which of course is Jesus Christ. He is the only true path who leads us back to the place of communion that Adam had with God before the Fall.

Finally, when there is a loss of communication in a specific area of our spiritual life, we must never curse the darkness, but compensate for our lack by developing other methods of perception. Like the deaf man who learns to hear through signing or the blind man who learns to see through touch, we must explore the many options of hearing and seeing available to us. If we properly utilize all of our senses, we will eventually awaken the latent powers of spiritual awareness that once enabled our ancestor Adam to hear and talk with the Creator.

# CHAPTER TWO

# Divine Appearances

**Now after He had risen early on the first day of the week, He first appeared to Mary Magdalene...**

**After that, He appeared in a different form to two of them while they were walking along on their way to the country (Mark 16:9,12).**

*I*T WAS AROUND MIDNIGHT ON A BRISK SEPTEMBER night. I was getting ready for bed and out of habit opened my bedroom window hoping to catch the cool, autumn breeze that blew gently through the trees in the backyard. I then settled beneath the sheets and positioned myself under the open window, eager to fall asleep with the smell of autumn in my nostrils. The sound of wind rustling through the fallen leaves on the ground and the occasional gust of air that blew through the open window was an added blessing to what I felt was a well-deserved night of rest.

I had just drifted off to sleep when I was awakened by the sound of leaves crunching under the feet of someone walking in the yard. Startled by the intrusion, my first reaction was one of fear as I remembered that a burglar had been terrorizing our neighborhood for the last several months. "Maybe this was the guy," I thought. "Should I get up and call the police, or just lie here and play dead?" Although I was not sure what to do, I knew I had only a few seconds to respond.

In spite of the urgency of the moment, I never had the chance to make my decision. As the sound of footsteps came closer and closer to my bedroom, the Spirit of the Lord began to fall upon me. In an instant, my fear gave way to a sense of reverent awe. "This is no burglar," I thought. "This is the Lord and He is coming to visit me. I must arise and present myself before Him."

As much as I wanted to get up and welcome Jesus, I could not find the strength to move a muscle. Instead, I lay there like a corpse—frozen with astonishment. Then, as if the Lord understood my dilemma, He turned the corner of the house and walked straight to my bedroom window. He stooped down, put the right cheek of His face against the screen that covered the open window, and without uttering a single word, He radiated the most warm, extraordinary love one could ever imagine.

Instantly, the room filled with the splendor of God's presence. At the same time, a radiant haze began to form in the atmosphere, hanging like a thick cloud over my bed. As the heavenly cloud descended on me, it seemed to be alive with the color red—the most vibrant, warm, living red that I had ever seen. Somehow, I knew that I was experiencing God's love in tangible form. As I began to breathe in this living cloud of tender affection, it seemed to penetrate every cell of my body. In a matter of minutes, I was completely intoxicated by the red cloud of love and felt as though I could not take in another ounce of His glorious presence.

For what seemed like a long time, the Lord stood at my window and bathed me with a revelation of His grace. I was made to understand that nothing could separate me from the immeasurable love of God in Christ Jesus—not life or death, principalities or powers, depth or height, or things present or things to come. I realized that Jesus is not only an awesome and mighty God, but He is also living Love, with a face. Regardless of my tendency to brokenness and failure, He loves me totally and unconditionally.

> I felt as though I could not take in another ounce of His glorious presence.

At that moment, I felt like my spirit was going to explode into a thousand pieces. To my surprise, however, there was more revelation in store for me that night. I had a strong impression that I was to focus on my hands. As I lifted my trembling hands up to my face, I felt as though I was seeing them for the first time. The soft but durable skin that was stretched over my bones, and the intricate lines engraved on the palm of my hands and fingers, told me that I was an extraordinary and complex work of creation. After a few seconds of bending and wiggling my fingers in utter fascination, I began to weep uncontrollably. I was overwhelmed with the revelation of Psalms 139:14 that I was awesomely and wonderfully made in the image of God.

At that point, the Lord interrupted my moment of discovery with a puzzling question. "Do you know why I put your hands on your arms?" Reluctantly I responded, "Lord I am not really sure. I think they are there to feed and care for myself and to touch and feel things, but I am sure there is more You want to show me."

The Lord replied, "I have given you hands as an expression of My heart. Since I am no longer visible in this physical world, you must be My hands extended. I want you to do what I would do if I were there in person. Use your hands to heal, comfort, embrace, affirm, and encourage people. Be gentle; never hit, push, or shove people with your hands, and never use your hands to clutch in greed. Always remember that your hands are made for releasing and giving. They are divine instruments of love and healing, and when you reach out to touch others, there will be times when it will seem as though your hands are literally My hands."

> It was also clear that all things in this world pale in comparison to the brightness of His glory.

After several minutes of this penetrating revelation, the Lord turned and walked away from my window without saying another word. I was disappointed He was leaving, but at the same time I was anxious to ponder the enormity of my visitation. I was not sure where this encounter would lead me in life, but I was certain that "Love" had visited my house. It was also clear that all things in this world pale in comparison to the brightness of His glory. Men, ministries, miracles, spiritual gifts, and other supernatural phenomena are all secondary to the splendor of the matchless One.

## Godly Appearances

Manifestations of Christ are known in theological terms as "Christophanies." Other manifestations known as "Theophanies" are similar in nature, but characterize the physical appearances of a deity—especially the persons of the Godhead. Some believe these manifestations are God taking on human form and interacting with His creation. Others believe they are intangible apparition, like visions and trances, but much stronger.

I am not sure how to classify my visitation, other than to say that it was as real as anything I have ever experienced. Whether or not it was a true Christophany does not change the fact that I encountered the Lord in the physical realm of sight, sound, and touch. It seemed as though I could reach out and touch His face.

Manifestations of this kind are clearly documented in Scripture and were experienced by people throughout the history of Judaism and Christianity. Abraham and Sarah, for example, encountered a Theophany in the later years of their lives. In Genesis 18, they were visited by three men who, after dining with the elderly couple, told Sarah she would shortly conceive a son. One of the men revealed to Abraham that He was "the Lord" and told him about the imminent destruction of the neighboring towns of Sodom and Gomorrah (see Genesis 18:17).

Manifestations of Christ were also alive in the New Testament. After the death and resurrection of Jesus, there were numerous appearances to His disciples. According to Mark 16:14, He appeared to eleven of them as they were eating together and commissioned them to preach the gospel to all nations. He also appeared to Peter in John 21:12; and in Luke 24:36, He appeared once more to all the disciples and rebuked them for their unbelief.

Other accounts of manifestations were also recorded in the New Testament—the most familiar being Christ's appearance to John on the Isle of Patmos. This disciple was privileged to see the glory of the resurrected Christ and wrote about the experience in a manuscript, known as the book of Revelation. John's description of the risen Lord in the first chapter has mesmerized readers for nearly two thousand years.

## Veiled Manifestations

Is it possible to be visited by Christ in physical form and not know it at the time? Such was the case of Mary Magdalene when she unknowingly encountered the risen Christ at His tomb in John 20:15. When Jesus tried to console her, she thought He was the caretaker of the garden and asked Him where they had taken the body of her Lord. When He addressed her by name, she then recognized Him and later announced to the disciples, **"...I have seen the Lord..." (John 20:18).**

Also, two men traveling on the Emmaus Road in Luke 24:15-50 encountered the Lord without recognizing who

He was. As they walked and talked about the current events that had transpired in Jerusalem, Jesus joined them and began a lengthy conversation about the things concerning Himself in Scripture. Later, when they invited Him into their house to eat, their eyes were opened to His true identity. He then vanished from their sight (see Luke 24:31).

Like these two incidents, I believe it is possible to be visited by Christ and not recognize Him at the time. There are numerous manifestations of this kind being reported around the world today. In some instances there is an immediate recognition of the Lord, like my experience as a young man. In other cases, unfortunately, it takes months or years before the person realizes they were visited by God.

Perhaps the most disturbing possibility is that we can have supernatural encounters and never know it until we get to heaven. Because of our spiritual blindness, we can easily stumble through life like a blind man who is incapable of recognizing the person standing in front of them. It is imperative, therefore, that we believe Jesus wants to have an encounter with us and that we walk in a place of awareness that will accommodate this kind of phenomenon. Remember that the essence of dead religion is trying to live the Christian life without experiencing the person of Christ.

## The Unveiling

What can we do to welcome divine manifestations into our lives? There are several interesting dynamics related to the experiences of Mary Magdalene and the two men on the Emmaus Road which are relevant to this question.

It is important to note that Mary Magdalene was a woman consumed with passion for the welfare of Jesus. Her soul was broken by the rejection and agony He suffered at the hands of those He was sent to save. It was only after she pleaded to know the whereabouts of the Lord's body that He revealed Himself to her. In my opinion, it was her deep affection for Jesus that caused Him to remove the veil of secrecy which separated them.

The two disciples on the Emmaus Road also encountered the Lord during a time of great curiosity and hunger for the things of God. According to Luke 24:31, their eyes were opened to His true identity when they welcomed Him as a stranger into the privacy of their home and served Him. Unknowingly, they had fulfilled Jesus' admonition in Matthew 23:3, that we cannot see Him until we receive those whom He has sent to us.

CHAPTER THREE

# Angels

**And the angel said unto them, Fear not; for behold, I bring you good tidings of great joy, which shall be to all people (Luke 2:10 KJV).**

*I*N THE SPRING OF 1985, I WAS DESPERATELY seeking God about His geographical will for my life. There were several options open to me at the time, but I was not sure which location was right. One night while praying about the matter, I fell asleep shortly after midnight. Several hours later, I was awakened with the sense of God's presence in the room.

At that instant, I entered a multi-dimensional state of consciousness. Like the apostle Paul in II Corinthians 12:2, I was not sure if I was in my body or out of my body. I was only aware that I was physically lying in my bedroom, while at the same time viewing the United States from a very great height. From this vantage point, I could see the outline of the West Coast.

Then to my surprise, an angel appeared at my right side and pointed to the coastline of California. The angel declared in a strong voice, "This is where God wants you. Obey God and live. Disobey God, and you will die." These words were repeated two more times and then the angel disappeared.

Needless to say, I was highly motivated to obey the words of the angel. Within a few months, I sold what few possessions I had, and said farewell to a bewildered group of family members and friends. Shortly afterward, I packed my family into our little car and drove away with $500 in my pocket and thirteen hundred miles to travel. To complicate matters, there was no job or ministry awaiting my arrival. All I possessed was faith in God and the generosity of an old friend who had called the night after my angel encounter to offer me temporary housing if I ever thought about moving to Southern California.

Little did my friend know the important timing of his phone call. When I called him back and told him I would be there in a few days, I am sure he was having second thoughts about his invitation. However, after arriving in the Los Angles area and spending a short season at his house, the Lord began to bless my act of obedience. I soon had a substantial income and was able to rent a house of my own. As each month passed, I began to reap the blessing of obedience, which had led me to the land of my anointing.

In spite of this success, I was still without a clear word as to the specific direction of my ministry. Then one afternoon as I was praying in my backyard, I once again felt the presence of a divine being behind me. As I turned around, I was face to face with an angel who I perceived was a "war angel." He was much larger and more authoritative than the "messenger angel" I had seen in the past. He was a fierce-looking angel and gripped a gigantic sword that was raised in a battle position over his head. He began to tell me that he was sent from God to war against the spirit of pride that wanted to lift up its head in the decade of the nineties.

He continued to say, "Humble yourself before God! Put your head down and keep a low profile. Heads are going to roll, for I have been commissioned to cut off the head of any man and ministry that is lifted up in pride. Remember that pride always comes before a fall."

To this day, I still remember the icy feeling in my veins and the goose bumps that ran up and down my body. For nearly a year after the visitation, I walked around slightly bent over in a posture of humility. As a result, I made it through the nineties with my ministry intact, whereas, several of my friends lost their ministries and their lives.

## Angels on Assignment

What are angels? According to contemporary theology, angels are celestial beings created by God before the beginning of time. They are spirits of wind-like velocity that have superhuman power and knowledge. In both the Hebrew and Greek language, they are depicted as ambassadors of God and divine couriers sent to instruct, inform, and occasionally command human beings. Angels also function as heavenly warriors and protective guardians.

No doubt there are various ranks, thrones, and principalities in the angelic kingdom. It is my opinion, however, that the Bible reveals three different classes of angelic beings. They are seraphim, cherubim, and angels. Of the three, seraphim and cherubim seem to be the least common. Other than Ezekiel, Isaiah, and John, there is no record of men ever interacting with these two groups of angels. Little is known about them, other than the cherubim have four wings and four faces, whereas, the seraphim have six wings and one face. Both are dedicated to the throne of God and seem to be guardians of His glory (see Ezekiel 1:5-12 and Revelation 4:8).

> Angels are spirits of wind-like velocity that have superhuman power and knowledge.

The function and behavior of angels, on the other hand, are clearly seen throughout the Bible. Although their dwelling place is in heaven, these angels often interact with mankind. The writers of Psalm 34:7 and Luke 16:22 inform us that they encamp around those who fear God and carry away the souls of the righteous to a place of rest. In Exodus 23:20, they guide men and nations to their destiny, and according to Matthew 18:10 and Exodus 32:34, their guardianship includes everything from little children to entire nations. Also, angels are seen fighting against the forces of evil in Revelation 12:7, and, according to Luke 15:10, they rejoice in the triumph of good and will appear with Christ at His second coming.

Generally speaking, I believe the bulk of angelic activity today can be divided into three categories—ambassadorship, warfare, and guardianship. The angel Gabriel for instance, who announced the good news of Christ's birth in the Gospels, was of the messenger class of angel. Michael the archangel, on the other hand, typifies the warring class of angel found in the book of Revelation. In Daniel 6:22, it was a guardian angel that surrounded and protected the prophet Daniel while imprisoned in a lions' den.

In view of the divine assignments of angels, we must be careful how we interact with these heavenly beings. Never disrespect or argue with a warring angel; trust the protection of guardian angels; and always obey the declaration of a messenger angel. In each case, your life could depend on the proper response to their presence.

When distinguishing between angels, also bear in mind that the Bible warns us about evil angels. According to II Peter 2:4 and Jude 6, there are fallen angels who have left their first estate and dwell in darkness. The apostle Paul also states in II Corinthians 11:14 that Satan can transform himself into an **"angel of light"** in an attempt to deceive those who are undiscerning.

In spite of this deception, believers should not live in a state of fear. God is faithful to lead us into all truth and will protect us from the deceitfulness of the devil. In my own life, I have learned that one of the primary roles of the Holy Spirit is to help me train my senses to discern between good and evil. For this reason, we are instructed in I John 4:1 to test any spirit that we encounter, to see if it comes from God.

## Angels Among Us

In addition to the activity of the angelic beings previously discussed, there are other characteristics relative to angels. In II Kings 6:17, angels are depicted as being invisible to the natural eye. According to Isaiah 6:6, they also fly through the heavens, creating a stir in both the spirit and natural world.

For example, just as a gust of invisible wind can stir the atmosphere around us, the movement of angels in the unseen world can set things into motion in the physical world. This activity is often detected as an unusual sound or the feeling of wind around your body or face. In some instances, you might also see a momentary flash of light out of the corner of your eye or shimmering colors that come and go around you. Whichever the case, we must learn to properly discern the presence of these heavenly beings and accommodate their purpose for being in our midst.

Angels can also manifest in the visible realm and are represented in Scripture as appearing in human form and having human characteristics. They can look like men, speak like men, and often take on the appearance of friends or strangers. The odds are great, therefore, that angels come and go throughout our lives on a frequent basis. Hebrews 13:2 says it is possible to entertain angels without knowing it.

Apparently, it was no stretch of the imagination for a first century Christian to believe that angels could take on the form of people they knew. Such was the case in Acts 12:13-15, when a group of disciples thought that the recently imprisoned Peter, who was knocking on their door, was a heavenly messenger. Although a servant girl named Rhoda recognized the apostle's voice, those gathered in the house insisted that it was not Peter, but his angel that was standing outside the door of the gate.

What does this say to us? There is little doubt that we unknowingly interact with angels on some level or another. I also believe these manifestations come to us in both male and female form. I am aware, of course, that many Bible teachers believe there is no gender difference in heaven. The fact remains that angels have the ability to take on any characteristic they choose, even the voice and form of a female.

> Angels can manifest in the visible realm and take on human form and characteristics.

On one occasion, I was visited by an angel who had the most authoritive, yet gentle female voice I had ever heard. The angel prophesied over me and instructed me with wisdom. I was later reminded of the verse in Proverbs 9:1 that states, **"Wisdom has...hewn out *her* seven pillars."** I also discovered in Proverbs 1:20-21 that, **"Wisdom calls aloud outside; *she* raises her voice in the open squares. *She* cries out at the chief concourses, at the opening of the gates in the city *she* speaks her words"** (NKJV).

## No More Harps

When interacting with angels it is necessary to keep an open mind. The spirit realm is a vast place of unexplored phenomena, and with the passing of every day we are drawing closer to encounters with the supernatural. Due to the lateness of the hour, God is slowly pulling back the veil of blindness that has kept us from seeing clearly into the spirit realm.

In no way, therefore, should we let religious tradition and myth keep us from a divine encounter with heaven. We must reconsider our image of lazy angels who float around on puffy white clouds playing golden harps. The silly myths of cute little cupids and chubby baby angels also have to go. We must learn to respect angels as divine beings from another world and recognize that they occasionally appear in human form.

However, this does not mean that we should embrace all spiritual manifestations just because they appear to be angelic, nor should we esteem created beings above the Creator. Bear in mind that there is a critical line which separates the worship of God from the worship of His creation. To put it bluntly, it is foolish to worship angels, but equally foolish to ignore them.

CHAPTER FOUR

# Visions

**"Then thou speakest in vision to thy saints..." (Psalm 89:19 ASV).**

THROUGHOUT MY LIFE I HAVE EXPERIENCED A number of supernatural visions. Several of these encounters lasted for what seemed like a long period of time; others were momentary glimpses into the spirit world of angels and demons. In either event, I have been privileged to see into the realm of the unseen.

One of the most profound of these visions came at the beginning of my ministry. It was Wednesday night in the month of October and I was snuggled tightly under my blanket, anticipating a warm night of rest. I had just drifted off to sleep when I was suddenly awakened by the presence of the Lord in the room. Immediately, I went into a three-dimensional vision that was astonishingly vivid. Within a matter of seconds, my whole being was overcome by a sensation of weightlessness that made my skin tingle from head to toe.

Then, like a leaf gently carried away by a gust of wind, my spirit slipped out of my body and ascended upward to the top of the ceiling and hovered over my bed. As I looked down at the lifeless form beneath me, I was struck with the realization that I was about to have a third heaven encounter with God. And, like the apostle Paul in II Corinthians 12:3, I was not quite sure if this experience was happening in or out of my body.

Within seconds, however, I was hurled in the vision through time and space where I landed on my hands and knees on an enormous marble courtyard. Now completely overtaken with the awe of my encounter, I fell prostrate on the surface of the gigantic floor, shaking with reverent fear. I realized that I was in the courtyard of heaven lying face down before the throne of Almighty God. Even more astonishing, there was no sound except what I can only describe as the sound of golden silence described in Revelation 8:1. The atmosphere was so thick with God's glory that nothing needed to be said, other than to acknowledge that the omnipotent God is seated on His throne, ruling in the affairs of men and angels.

> God is eager to communicate with His creation through visions.

I am not sure how long I lay before the Lord that night in the vision. However, when I did return to a conscious state of mind, there was a sense that something incredible had been downloaded into my spirit and that it would carry me through the turbulent storms of life that lay ahead. The time spent before God in the vision seemed to be both my commissioning into prophetic office and the assurance that the Lord would cause me to succeed in that ministry.

From that day forward, I intuitively knew the value of my calling and the meaning of my destiny. Furthermore, I learned that God is eager to communicate with His creation through visions, even though we are unfamiliar with such an advanced form of communication. I also discovered several years later that visions can be counterfeited by the "powers of darkness" and without the discernment and protection of the Holy Spirit, we run the risk of being deceived by a false **"angel of light."**

In one particular vision, for example, an evil angel appeared in front of me, much like the account in Zechariah 3:1, and delivered a prophecy that was completely different from what God had revealed to me in the past. The words spoken were indeed powerful, but tainted with deception and false information that was filtered through a second heaven revelation.

Apparently, I had engaged the dark side of the spirit world and was presented with the negative plans of Satan for my life. Although I was crippled by this experience for a period of time, I soon learned to distinguish between second heaven and third heaven revelation—a subject that will be briefly explained later in this chapter.

## Visions of Grandeur

According to the *Strong's Concordance*, the root meaning for the word "vision" is "to perceive or see."

*Unger's Bible Dictionary* also defines "visions" as a "supernatural presentation of scenery or circumstances to the mind of a person while awake." Other references suggest that visions are inspired insights of revelation from God.

My understanding of visions is much the same. I believe there are times when natural perception gives way to supernatural imagery. While awake, one can see heavenly scenes superimposed over one's eyes and mind. Like the servant of Elijah, whose eyes were opened to a host of angels in II Kings 6:17, the Lord can open our spiritual vision to see things that are undetectable at the time. Sometimes these images are momentary; at other times they can last for a long time.

Such visions were common throughout church history and are mentioned over one hundred times in the Bible. In the Old Testament, visions were experienced by men such as Abraham, Balaam, Samuel, Isaiah, Ezekiel, Habakkuk, and Daniel. In the New Testament, men like Zacharias, Peter, James, Paul, and John also testified to seeing visions. The apostle Paul also received numerous visions throughout his ministry. And, the apocalyptic vision given to John the beloved is contained solely in the book of Revelation (see Genesis 15:1, Numbers 24:4, Isaiah 1:1, Ezekiel 11:24, Daniel 4:13, Habakkuk 2:2, Luke 1:22, Matthew 17:9, Acts 11:5, Acts 16:9, and Revelation 9:17).

Like these Bible characters, people today are experiencing visions. It is not uncommon for contemporary Christians to have supernatural visions of heaven, hell, angels, and even God Himself. Through these visions, many have obtained secret information about the plans of God for nations and governments. Others have received insight into the realm of wicked principalities and are able to diffuse the satanic strategy that is designed to cause chaos and destruction.

A great number of people also have visions that contain warnings, predictions, and other prophetic messages. Because of these visions, many are informed about things to come, such as shifting economic trends, changing weather patterns, and other events related to our everyday lives. In the recent past, my friend, Bob Jones, has had several visions about unusual weather storms, long before they devastated parts of this nation.

## Hosting a Vision

Although visions are a part of our spiritual experience, be advised that not all visions are from God. This means we must verify the source of our vision and be cautious of what many today call "second heaven revelation." It is taught that there are three heavens—the first being the physical heavens, the second being a spiritual realm where fallen angels and principalities abide, and the third being the highest spiritual realm where God lives.

Why is the distinction of these realms important to the issue of visions?

It is necessary to point out that the second heaven is described in Ephesians 2:2 as a place where Satan rules as **"the prince of the power of the air."** In this spiritual domain, the intent and purpose of the enemy can be picked up and misconstrued as being from God.

This truth is especially important to visionaries and prophetic intercessors, who occasionally tap into the second heaven and mistakenly interpret and apply the revelation they receive as though it were God's will. As a result, the plans of the dark side are often prophesied and prayed over people and churches, causing great distress.

As indicated, the third heaven should be the true source of our revelation. The apostle Paul, for example, wrote about a third heaven experience in II Corinthians 12:4, and said that he was caught up into paradise and heard inexpressible things that were impossible to utter. It is not clear whether he was able to capture the event with the human tongue or if he was unable to fully understand its meaning. In either event, he seemed to struggle with the interpretation and application of his vision.

> Visions were common occurrences throughout church history and are mentioned over one hundred times in the Bible.

As with Paul, the fact that we can have a third heaven experience does not always mean we have the proper interpretation. Therefore, we must consider the following questions. Is the vision literal, symbolic, or cryptic? Does it apply to you personally or to someone else? Is it connected to the past, present, or future? Is the message obvious, or does it have a hidden meaning? Should the vision be a matter of personal prayer, or do you announce it to everyone? Only you and the Holy Spirit can determine the answer to these questions.

## Conclusion

How do we expand our capacity to receive visions? And how can we properly interpret and apply these heavenly images?

First, I believe prayer, praise, fasting, Bible meditation, and other spiritual disciplines are closely related to our ability to receive from God. All of these dynamics have a soothing effect on the human soul and seem to sensitize our spirit to the supernatural. It is interesting to note that many visions in the Bible occurred during or right after times of spiritual devotion.

Next, we must fight through the treacherous domain of the second heaven in our prayer and praise time, and reach out for third heaven experiences. This means we have to press into the throne room of God, regardless of our lack of time and patience. As in the case of the prophet Daniel, determination and persistence will eventually open the door to heavenly visitations (see Daniel 10:14).

Finally, make an attempt to write or record your vision. It may not seem important or have much meaning at the time, but later when you begin the process of interpretation you will need to remember it accurately. Also, a third heaven vision needs to be recorded for the benefit of others. The author of Habakkuk 2:2 declares, **"Record the vision and inscribe it on tablets, that the one who reads it may run."**

# CHAPTER FIVE

# Trances

**"And it came to pass, that, when I had returned to Jerusalem, and while I prayed in the temple, I fell into a trance" (Acts 22:17 ASV).**

IT WAS LATE SUMMER, AND I HAD JUST ARRIVED AT my home following a Sunday night church service. As I reached to open the car door, I was instantly caught up into a trance. At that moment, I was not quite sure if I was in or out of my body. However, in a matter of seconds it was increasingly clear that I was in the presence of God, about to experience things too difficult to understand with the human mind.

Like the glow of a giant, neon light, everything around me turned a fluorescent shade of blue. Intuitively, I knew two things about this heavenly blue color. First, I was seeing the cloud of Shekinah glory found in the Old Testament and it was alive with the awe and wonder of God. Second, this supernatural cloud of shimmering blue seemed to be coming from the mouth of God. On the one hand, it was beautiful and inviting. On the other hand, it was awesomely chilling, like the vapors of frosty air that are released when breath is exhaled on a crisp, winter morning.

This phenomenon seemed to penetrate every molecule in the universe, including the smallest particle of dust in distant galaxies. Like a giant blanket, it covered the past, present, and future. Shrinking back in my seat, I covered my mouth, too afraid to move or breathe. I was terrified at the thought of contaminating the Spirit of God with human breath. For a moment, I wanted to stop breathing forever.

Just as I was about to recover from the shock of this encounter, something more dramatic began to happen.

> It is nearly impossible to maintain a humble prayer life and not encounter the supernatural on one level or another.

I saw God sitting above the circle of the universe, on a throne of unearthly origin and design. As the Lord slowly turned His head in my direction, the universe seemed to turn on its axis with Him. I then realized He was about to focus His full attention upon me. In the same way that earth and heaven fled from the Lord's face in Revelation 20:11, I was also looking for a place to hide from His piercing gaze.

Even so, there was no escaping my moment of encounter with God. With one penetrating look, His eyes cut through the thoughts and intents of my heart and down to the marrow of my bones. Like a mighty sword, it divided asunder my spirit, soul, and body. There was nowhere to run or hide. Every cell in my body trembled in fear and cried out for the rocks and mountains to hide me from **"...the face of Him who sits on the throne..." (Revelation 6:16 NKJV).**

By this time, I was totally undone, disoriented, and most of all in a deep state of emotional shock. For the first time, I understood the paralyzing fear of the Lord that was experienced by John, Abraham, Daniel, and other men of God in the Bible. I was so intoxicated with the awe of God that I staggered like a drunken man, unable to walk through the door of my house. For hours I could not hold my head up straight or control the muscles in my body. Similar to the author of Revelation 1:17, I was reeling from the effects of a spiritual manifestation that left me weak and breathless. To this day, the memory of my experience leaves me smitten with the awe of God (see Genesis 15:12, Daniel 8:27, and Revelation 1:17).

### Daydreams or Trances?

What are trances? The Greek word for "trance" literally means "standing outside one's normal state of mind." In a nutshell, trances are a displacement of the mind which gives a person a sense of detachment from their physical surroundings. While in this state, the mind and senses will often shut down, allowing the person to be overtaken by visual images. As a rule, these trances are similar to visions, but stronger in intensity and longer in duration of time.

As with visions and dreams, however, not all trances are congruent with the Spirit of God. Many self-induced trances come as a result of intense concentration of the mind, thoughtless meditation, or the abuse of certain drugs. People that experience trances of this nature are usually not conscious of outward impressions and are wrapped in a world of vain imagination.

Biblical trances, on the other hand, are not to be confused with a hypnotic state where you stare off into space, empty-headedly. Neither can we make them happen by closing our eyes and trying to work up a spiritual experience. Actually, the spiritual authenticity of a biblical trance is marked by the witness of either seeing or hearing from God.

In Acts 10:10, for example, Peter fell into a trance while praying on a rooftop and heard God speak to him concerning His benevolence to the Gentiles. The apostle Paul also fell into a trance while praying in Acts 22:17 and was instructed by the risen Christ to quickly leave the city of Jerusalem. Other men of God in the Bible experienced the phenomenon of trances, such as the time when Abraham fell into a trance in Genesis 15:12 and was told of things to come. In Numbers 24:4, the prophet Balaam also heard God's voice while in a trance; and in Ezekiel 3:15, the hand of Jehovah came upon the prophet Ezekiel after he sat for seven days in a trance-like state.

> Trances are a displacement of the mind, which gives a person a sense of detachment from their physical surroundings.

Trances are also evident in modern times. It is a known fact that people in the last several hundred years of Christianity have experienced biblical trances of incredible magnitude. Perhaps one of the most well-known cases was a female evangelist named Mary Woodworth-Etter, who lived during the turn of the twentieth century. She was known to go into trances and stand motionless for hours and occasionally days. It is reported that during these times people would come into her meetings, fall under the power of the Holy Spirit, and be miraculously healed or converted.

## The Prayer Connection

Most people believe that trances are sovereign manifestations of the Spirit and that little can be done on the human side to command them. On the contrary, I have found that the majority of Bible characters mentioned in this chapter did have one thing in common. They were praying when they fell into a trance. As stated earlier, Paul experienced this phenomenon while praying in a temple; Peter's trance came while praying on the roof of a house; and Abraham's trance came as he communed with God during a time of sacrificial offering.

This tells me that the primary connection to biblical trances is established through prayer and intercession. I believe this is partly due to the humility of heart brought about by this kind of devotion, which according to James 4:6, is God's grace given to the humble. I also believe it is nearly impossible to maintain a humble prayer life and not encounter the supernatural on one level or another.

In light of this truth, why do so many in the church miss such an important connection? In my opinion, the majority of believers become discouraged with prayer because they do not understand the spiritual dynamics that govern their prayer life. Little is known about the principle of sowing and reaping, and few in the church really comprehend that prayer is a seed that grows into spiritual fruit. Even more tragic is the false mentality that we can experience a great spiritual harvest without sowing generous seeds of prayer.

What farmer, for example, would sow sparingly and expect to see a record harvest? Or, what farmer would plant a crop and expect to see immediate results the next day or week?

The same is true of prayer and spiritual encounters with God. The seeds for a supernatural harvest are sown in earnest prayer, whereas the fruits are gathered at a later time. The author of II Corinthians 9:6 tells us **"...He that soweth sparingly shall reap also sparingly; and he that soweth bountifully shall reap also bountifully"** (ASV).

Such was the nature of my experience described at the beginning of this chapter. Before I encountered God in the trance, I had already spent a lot of time seeking Him in fervent prayer. I was so hungry for the supernatural that a week earlier I retreated to a solitary place in the forest and poured my heart out under the shade of a giant oak tree. This time of deep devotion and weeping was probably the seed that later blossomed into a full-blown trance.

## Conclusion

What can we do to maintain our prayer connection even when there seems to be little or no response from heaven?

Practically speaking, do not be discouraged. Pray and keep on praying. One day when you least expect it, an encounter with God will fall on you. It will happen—not because you deserve it, but because God is a good farmer and in time yields a return on every seed planted. It is His nature to multiply the seed sown way beyond your greatest expectations.

You must also exercise your faith and not give up on the fact that God wants to bless your life with supernatural manifestations. Remember that it was the relentless determination of the widow in Luke 18:5 that caused the judge to grant her request. In view of this principle, we, too, must ask and keep on asking; seek and keep on seeking; knock and keep on knocking. According to Matthew 7:7, if you continue to ask, it will be given to you; if you continue to seek you will find, and when you continually knock it will be opened to you.

# CHAPTER SIX

# Dreams

**Indeed God speaks once, or twice, yet no one notices it.**

**In a dream, a vision of the night, when sound sleep falls on men, while they slumber in their beds (Job 33:14-15).**

*I*N MY EARLY TWENTIES, I WAS PLAYING GUITAR IN a contemporary gospel band called "The Sounds of Joy." The five of us were preparing to make our first record and had just taken the photo for the album cover. Everything was in place and we were waiting with anticipation for our recording appointment at a studio in Nashville, Tennessee.

Several weeks before the event was scheduled, I had a dream that forever changed my life and ministry. In the dream, I was walking down a dirt road with the other four members of the band, talking and having fun. As we approached an old wooden bridge, I sensed that I could not cross over with them to the other side. My heart was sad, but I knew that my destiny lay somewhere else, in a place and time that I could not yet see or understand. In spite of my love for music and the other members of the band, I knew I must let go of my lifelong passion to become a professional musician and trust God for the future.

As I stood alone in the dream, something strange began to stir deep in my heart. I had a gut feeling to look up into the sky. As I gazed upward into the starry night, I was drawn to the seven stars that make up the Big Dipper. To my surprise, there was another dipper the same size as the first and they were facing each other at a forty-five degree angle, making fourteen stars in total. Each dipper contained a golden liquid that was semi-translucent, much like olive oil.

> Dreams are one of the ways God talks to people today.

Slowly, the dippers rotated in synchronization, like the hands of a giant clock moved by an unseen force. Then as the dippers tilted simultaneously over my head, the oil from each one came together into a single stream, pouring down from the night sky. As the stream of oil came crashing down on my head, an indescribable feeling of bliss ran down my face and body to the soles of my feet. When the dippers were empty, there appeared a dazzling white cane in the eastern sky, much like that of a shepherd's crook. I suddenly awoke from the dream ecstatic with joy, but bewildered by an apparent lack of interpretation.

For years I pondered the full meaning of the dream. It was obvious that I could no longer stay in the band, nor would I ever become a Christian recording artist. I also knew that the two dippers of oil represented the prophetic and teaching ministry that would be poured out onto my life as one stream of anointing. As I suspected, this ministry began shortly thereafter.

However, I was not sure about the other aspects of the dream. What did the fourteen stars represent, and what about the dazzling white cane? Were the fourteen stars that made up both dippers symbolic of future years, like the seven thin cows and seven fat cows in Pharaoh's dream in Genesis 41:20, which represented fourteen years of approaching prosperity and famine in Egypt? Did the cane speak of the biblical authority of a shepherd's staff? Did the white color of the cane represent righteousness and holiness like the garments of the saints in Revelation 19:14? I was not sure of the exact meaning, but I knew these things were important keys to my destiny.

As the years went by, the experience began to fade into the shadows of yesterday. Then in 1989, things took on a new meaning. While sitting in a meeting in Los Angeles, listening to an internationally known prophet, I suddenly realized that it was exactly fourteen years since I had received the dream. Even more amazing, the prophet speaking that night was Paul Cain, and he had the same hair color as the dazzling cane in the dream, which was pure white.

Things were finally beginning to make sense. After years of pioneering in prophetic ministry, divine providence had placed me in the presence of one of the great "prophetic ministries" of our time. In the following decade, I was blessed to develop a ministry association and friendship with the white cane (Cain), I had seen in my dream long ago. Even more valuable was his down-to-earth ministry style and gentle disposition, which served as a godly example to me and the ministers who grew up in an era that equated prophetic ministry with harshness and weirdness. As you would expect, I am thankful for a heavenly dream that declared the path I was to take long before I ever arrived.

## The Making of a Dream

Dreams are one of the ways God talked to people in the Bible. In the Old Testament, Jacob received blessing from God through a dream. Joseph was also given insight into his destiny as the result of a childhood dream. Pharaoh also received information about the future of Egypt in a dream, and Daniel saw the future events of the world in two consecutive dreams. In the New Testament, the angel of the Lord appeared to Joseph, the father of Jesus, in a dream. It was also in a dream that another angel instructed the apostle Paul concerning the fate of those who traveled with him on a voyage to Rome (see Genesis 28:12, 37:5, Daniel 7:1, Matthew 1:20, and Acts 27:23).

What is the true nature of such dreams? Is there a significant difference between ordinary dreams and the spiritual dreams just described?

Primarily, a natural dream is a series of images and ideas that occur during sleep. These dreams are connected to the physical and psychological state of a person, and their origin lies somewhere beneath the threshold of consciousness. A majority of these dreams seem to reflect events, thoughts, and feelings of the person dreaming. This dream content is also a mixture of current events, past experiences, hidden desires, thoughts, urges, and interests that relate to the life of the person. Such dreams have little spiritual significance, and as King Solomon stated in Ecclesiastes 5:3, they often come through a multitude of words.

Spiritual dreams, on the other hand, have many of the same characteristics as natural dreams, but are different in origin and meaning. Whereas, the natural dream comes from the mind and soul of a person, the spiritual dream seems to originate from deep within the spirit of mankind and carries specific messages from God. Even more interesting, the Spirit of God will often invade the realm of natural dreaming and download spiritual information and images, creating a mixture of soulish and spiritual imagery that must be carefully analyzed. In either event, both kinds of dreams should be properly interpreted and applied to our lives.

How do we accomplish this task? To discern between natural dreams and spiritual dreams, a simple test can be used. Does the dream provoke you to pray and seek God? Is there a sense of God's presence in the dream or immediately following the dream? While in the middle of the dream, do you become aware that the dream is from God? Is the dream repeated over and over again? Is the dream symbolic or cryptic by nature? Is Scripture seen or spoken in the dream? Do you awake abruptly from the dream with a sense of God's presence? Does the dream keep coming to your mind for days or weeks afterwards?

If you can say yes to any of these questions, there is a strong possibility that your dream is inspired by God. Again, you must bear in mind that both the natural and spiritual realm are at times intermingled in your dream life, making it difficult to sort out what is God and what is flesh. In spite of this, do not be discouraged, but begin to write down your dreams for future reference and pray over them. In due time, the Holy Spirit will teach you to separate the good from the bad.

## A Dream Come True

In addition to mystical dreams like the one about the Big Dipper, I have had hundreds of dreams that relate to the common and ordinary affairs of life. I have dreamed accurately about the rise and fall of the stock market, and have perceived upcoming seasons of prosperity for my life in a dream. I have had a number of other dreams regarding people I have yet to meet, and in one instance I dreamed about my marriage to Laura long before we started dating.

I have also dreamed about the birth of one of my grandchildren before my daughter was pregnant. I have also had several dreams about the death of friends and family members, long before they fell sick. Every now and then, I dream about the more practical aspects of life, like where to move, what to buy, and how to conduct myself in the presence of others.

Dreams have also served me in the delivery of my ministry. On numerous occasions, I have walked into the pulpit armed with secret information that I received in a dream the night before. As a result of these dreams, I am better equipped to meet the needs of people who come to my meetings.

In a recent example, while ministering on the East Coast, I dreamed I had called out a lady named Deborah Jean from the back row of a conference and encouraged her about the future of her five children. After awakening from the dream, I wrote the specific information down on my notepad and prepared for the evening meeting.

When I arrived at the conference, I was brought onto the stage in front of a large crowd that was jammed into a dimly lit room. In an act of obedience, I pointed to the spot where I dreamed the lady was sitting and said, "Deborah Jean, come forward; I have a message for you and your five children." Much to my relief the lady stood up, acknowledged her name and listened to the words of encouragement that I had received for her in the dream.

> After awakening from a dream, always write or record the dream.

In a letter that followed several months later, Deborah told me that she was greatly discouraged at that time and worried about the future of her children. The night of the conference she had decided to go to church for the last time seeking help, and if nothing happened, she was never going to return again. To say the least, she was thrilled that God knew her by name and that He was concerned about the welfare of her five children. She testified about making a new commitment to God and feeling a renewed sense of destiny for herself and her family.

## Dream Weavers

In addition to natural and spiritual dreams, we are also susceptible to dreams from the "dark side." Actually, there are hordes of strange spirits eager to invade our subconscious mind and torment us while dreaming. People who have a high level of sensitivity to the spirit world are especially at risk. For this reason, perceptive people should be careful where they sleep, such as seedy hotels or the bed of a person that has spiritual or emotional problems. Sometimes you can pick up a residue of negativity from people who have been there before you.

It is also important to monitor the atmosphere in your home. Be sure to turn off any negative television shows or movies before going to sleep. Just as important, you should never read sinister literature before bed or play depressing music before or during sleep. Again, your subconscious mind is susceptible to the spirit world and these things can creep into your dream life.

On a more constructive note, your dream life can also be affected in a positive manner. Before going to bed, keep your thoughts wholesome. Think on those things that are pure and good as Paul described in Philippians 4:8. Also, read your Bible before sleeping, and when possible, play soothing soundtracks of worship music or Scripture during sleep. I assure you that your dream life will radically change, and you will begin to have dreams of a spiritual nature.

CHAPTER SEVEN

# Audible Voice

**After being baptized, Jesus came up immediately from the water; and behold, the heavens were opened, and he saw the Spirit of God descending as a dove and lighting on Him,**

**and behold, a voice out of the heavens said, "This is My beloved Son, in whom I am well-pleased" (Matthew 3:16-17).**

*I*N MY LATE FORTIES, I WENT THROUGH A VICIOUS attack against my physical and mental health. Within a period of two years, I was mysteriously struck by partial blindness, unexplainable dizziness, memory loss, high blood pressure, panic attacks, severe rheumatoid arthritis, skin cancer, acute prostate and kidney infections, strange viruses, and heart palpitations which severely disrupted my life.

During this time, it seemed as though God was a million miles away. Every time someone prayed for me, the problem grew worse, not better. Frustrated and at the end of my rope, I turned to the medical community for help. Thank God they were able to relieve a portion of my suffering through therapy and medication.

Little did I know, however, that God would have to intervene in a most unusual way. It all began one night as I lay in bed pondering my dilemma. Out of nowhere, a wind blew through the open door of my bedroom and moved in close to my bed. The presence of the Holy Spirit suddenly filled the room and an audible voice said. "You shall live and not die." Then as quickly as it came, the wind departed.

Now I was really puzzled. If the Holy Spirit had to notify me in an audible voice that I was going to live and not die, I knew I was about to face a great challenge. As I suspected, I soon developed an irregular heartbeat that eventually turned into a racing heart of over 170 beats per minute. My family called 911 at my request, and by the time the ambulance arrived I was on the floor unable to breathe and losing consciousness. My heart was so erratic that the paramedics were unable to determine if I was having an actual heart attack or an episode of arterial fibrillation.

> We can increase our chances of hearing clearly by activating our faith and believing for verbal confirmation of God's presence.

After an unsuccessful diagnosis, I was strapped into the bed of the ambulance and whisked away to a local hospital. When I arrived at the emergency room, the doctors were able to get my heart rate down but could not stabilize the irregular beat. After several hours of examination, I was finally admitted to the hospital for further treatment.

The next morning, the heart specialist came into my room and told me they would have to stop and restart my heart in hopes of returning it to a normal rhythm. As the severity of my situation settled on me, a spirit of fear began to grip my mind. "This is probably going to kill me," I thought. Then I remembered what the audible voice had said to me the week before, and I began to repeat over and over, "I shall live and not die. I shall live and not die."

In that instance, my courage returned and laughter began to flow like a river from deep inside my belly. Several minutes later, I sat up on the edge of the bed and instantly my heart returned to its normal rhythm. When the nurse came to prepare me for more tests, she was surprised by my rapid recovery. I was discharged from the hospital later that morning, feeling as though nothing had happened. I still have occasional heart palpitations, but according to the audible voice of God, I shall live and not die until He is ready for me to go home.

## Demonic or Divine?

Mental institutions are filled with people who hear voices. In some cases, these voices are heard by those with brain disorders, those who are insane, or those who have abused themselves with drugs. I also believe many of these people hear audible voices that originate from the realm of spiritual darkness. Usually these voices are nothing more than evil spirits mimicking human speech.

In obedience to these diabolical voices, thousands of people have committed horrible acts of violence. They have been instructed to torture, rape, murder, and even take their own lives. To complicate matters, these wicked spirits often insist that their commands are the voice of God. Oftentimes, those who yield to these delusions are not only convinced they hear from God, but also believe they themselves are God.

In spite of these demonic proclamations, not all supernatural voices are from the "dark side." There are many people today who truly hear from God and are led by His audible voice. If Satan can speak into the natural realm, then certainly the Creator of all things can speak audibly to His creation.

> Not all supernatural voices are from the "dark side." There are people today who truly hear from God and are led by His audible voice.

Such was the case throughout the Bible. In Genesis 1:3, the Almighty spoke to the empty void of space and said, **"Let there be light."** In another example in Daniel 4:31, the voice of God fell from heaven on Nebuchadnezzar and advised the king about his tragic fate. The audible voice of God likewise fell at the baptism of Jesus in Matthew 3:17 and declared, **"This is My beloved Son, in whom I am well-pleased."** This same voice was also heard on the Mount of Transfiguration in Matthew 17:5.

In a literal sense, the Lord is also speaking audibly to people today. My wife Laura tells of an unusual experience with the audible voice of God that kept her from serious harm.

At the age of fifteen, she and a girlfriend had decided to go to the movies on a rainy night in La Habra, California. After the movie, they were hungry and stopped by an outdoor taco stand to pick up some food. As they faced the order board with their backs to the street, they were unaware of the dangerous condition that existed on the slick road behind them.

While ordering her food, Laura suddenly heard an audible voice that said, "Move now!" Instinctively, she grabbed her friend and pushed her away from the taco stand where they both fell into a row of trash cans. In her head she was thinking, "I had better have a good reason for pushing my girlfriend who is wearing a mini-dress into a trash can." Just as she had completed the thought, she heard a loud noise and noticed bits of glass bouncing off her hair and clothing.

Apparently, a car traveling down the street behind them had spun out of control and crashed into the taco stand where they were standing. Needless to say, the girls were shaken up a bit, but not seriously injured. Had Laura not obeyed the voice of warning, however, they would have suffered serious injury if not death. Laura recently told me she was not sure if the words came from God or an angel, but she knew that she and her friend had been protected from harm by heeding an audible voice from heaven.

## Voice Lessons

I believe experiences like those described in this chapter will increase in the near future. This is partly due to the desire of believers to receive from God and the demand the church has put on heaven to hear the voice of the Bridegroom. I am not saying we can force the Lord to speak audibly to us by praying demanding prayers or offering up defiant intercession. I do believe, however, that there are lessons we can learn that will increase our chances of hearing clearly.

First, it is possible to activate our faith and believe for verbal confirmation of God's presence. This seemed to be the case in II Chronicles 1:6, when God spoke to King Solomon after he had offered up a thousand sacrifices unto the Lord. Perhaps Solomon was motivated by the words of his father David in Psalm 91:15 which declares that we can call out to God and He will answer us in our time of need.

Next, the audible voice of God that fell at Jesus' baptism was heaven's response to a life that brought praise to the Father. I know it is a stretch of biblical interpretation, but this passage seems to indicate that if we want to hear good things from heaven, we must give God something to talk about. In simple terms, it is possible to invoke a reply from heaven by the very nature of our conduct.

## Proper Perspective

Be advised that hearing the voice of God also requires the responsibility of obeying the voice of God. It would be better not to hear God at all than to hear and disobey. Why? Because this level of disobedience is equivalent to the sin of rebellion, and according to I Samuel 15:23 it will invoke the judgment of God. As an act of mercy, therefore, He would rather say nothing to us than have us suffer the penalty of disobedience.

In light of this danger, seasons of silence from God could be a blessing in disguise. So, do not be discouraged; just be aware that there are times when God may be saying much more than you really want to hear or obey. Also, take into consideration that God wants to speak *through you* as much as He wants to speak *to you*.

# CHAPTER EIGHT

# Inner Voice and Conscience

**...but the LORD was not in the earthquake:**

**And after the earthquake a fire but the LORD was not in the fire; and after the fire a still small voice (I Kings 19:11-12 KJV).**

EVERAL YEARS AGO, I WAS AWAKENED FROM SLEEP by the sound of a voice speaking to me. "Be careful," the voice urged, "Stay alert and look both ways tomorrow."

At first I thought there was someone in the room, but soon discovered that the words were coming from deep inside my spirit. Although the voice was not quite audible, it was stronger than any impression I had ever encountered. Intuitively, I knew this was the inner voice of the Lord and I should pay attention.

As you would expect, I was perplexed regarding the precise meaning of this warning. As I pondered the experience, my mind drifted back to a story my father told me as a young boy. Several times, Dad had described in detail how his life had been saved by what he called the inner voice of God. While working at a mining company in Bauxite, Arkansas, he was instructed by a voice to avoid a particular truck assigned to him. Against company policy, he got on another truck and rode it out of the mine. To make a long story short, the truck Dad was originally assigned to ride in plunged down a cliff, killing everyone. Had my father ignored the inner voice of God's Spirit, he would have also died that day.

If my dad's life was spared by heeding the inner voice of God, I thought then perhaps God was also warning me about some impending danger. With this in mind, I awoke the following morning determined to stay alert. I exercised extreme caution everywhere I went. When driving, I closely monitored the traffic on the right and left of every intersection. When walking, I never stepped off a curb without looking down both ways of the street. At the end of the day, I returned home assuming I had fulfilled the word of the Lord.

> The voice of conscience is God's implant—the oracle of right and wrong.

Confident that any threat of danger had passed, I left my house that night and drove to the church I was pastoring. After the meeting ended, I visited with several people and got into my car, eager to make the five mile trip back home.

On the last leg of the trip, I had to stop in the middle of a busy two-lane highway and wait for a break in the approaching traffic before turning onto my street. As I sat with my blinker on, waiting to make the left-hand turn, I was once again reminded of the warning from the night before. Out of sheer instinct, I looked one more time to my right and left and then decided for some reason to look behind me.

When I fixed my eyes on the rearview mirror, my heart nearly stopped. I could see the headlights of a truck coming up behind me at a high rate of speed. Apparently, the driver did not have time to avoid my car, much less the time to stop. I was as helpless as a sitting duck and had only a few precious seconds to make a life and death decision.

In spite of the sudden panic, I quickly evaluated the situation and decided on a course of action. I was aware that my wheels were turned to the left and on impact I would be catapulted into the stream of oncoming traffic and crushed to death. My only chance for survival was to turn my wheels in the opposite direction and hope that the impact would push me off the road and away from the traffic. In those final seconds, before the truck exploded into the rear of my car, I managed to spin the steering wheel to the right. As I had calculated, the force of impact pushed me several hundred feet down the right side of the highway where my car finally flipped over on its top and came to rest in a ditch. Miraculously, I walked away with only a minor bump on the back of my head.

## Conscience and Still, Small Voice

As discussed in the previous chapter, people in Bible days often heard the audible voice of God in the natural realm of hearing. Although believers today can also hear in this fashion, the most common method of hearing is by the inner voice of God. Like my experience with the accident, it is hearing an inner voice or feeling an inner witness that often instructs us in the way we should go.

What is this inner voice and where exactly does it come from? Is it the voice of the Holy Spirit speaking to the human spirit, or is it the presence of the Holy Spirit bearing witness to the voice of conscience?

I believe the human conscience is in some ways synonymous with the voice of the Holy Spirit. This is apparent when you consider that the conscience of man is God's implant—the oracle of right and wrong. Basically, conscience is a person's inner awareness of conforming to the will of God or departing from it, resulting in a sense of what is correct and incorrect in one's conduct or motives.

Although the term "conscience" does not appear in the Old Testament, the concept does. David, for example, was smitten in his heart in II Samuel 24:10 because of his lack of trust in God's power. In the New Testament, Paul also writes about the issue of conscience and declares that we are led by a sanctified conscience as the Holy Spirit bears witness. He clearly stated in Romans 9:1 that the testimony of his conscience was pure and honest, primarily because the Holy Spirit was present to validate it in the truth.

As to the nature and expression of conscience, it is similar to the impressions and spiritual perception we will discuss in the next chapter, but quite different than the audible voice of God previously described. It is often manifested as an inner witness, a soothing feeling, a sense of peace, a feeling of affirmation, or the smallest prick of our conscience. In some cases, this phenomenon is so real that it actually sounds like a still, small voice.

The same was true of the prophet Elijah. When he encountered the Lord on the mountain where Moses had earlier experienced the audible voice of the Lord, the prophet quickly discovered that God was not speaking to him in the same way. At that moment in time, Elijah could not find God either in the radiance of the fire, the sound of the wind, or the noise of the earthquake. He did, nonetheless, hear the still, small voice of the Lord when he wrapped his face in the skirts of his robe to block out the noise around him (see I Kings 19:11-13).

> Like the sound of a trumpet lost in the noise of battle, the Holy Spirit can be drowned out by the turbulent clamor of the human soul.

Like Elijah, we must recognize that we cannot encounter God on another man's mountain experience. As I have indicated throughout this book, we are unique individuals and hear God's voice in many different ways. For some, this means that the inner voice of the Spirit is actually God communicating through their conscience. Others perceive it as the Spirit of God bearing witness with their spirit, while others believe it is the literal voice of the Holy Spirit speaking to their mind and spirit.

Whichever the case, I am convinced that God speaks to us through inner declarations of His Spirit. I also believe these whispers of the Spirit are given to encourage the downhearted, provide instruction to those lacking wisdom, and give direction to people in need of guidance. As I stated earlier, the inner voice of God protected me and my father from great danger.

## Busy Signal!

How do we cultivate this aspect of spiritual hearing? Are there things we can do to sensitize our spirits to the inner voice of God?

Long ago, I learned that a busy mind is a hindrance to hearing the still, small voice of God. Like the sound of a trumpet that is lost in the noise of battle, the voice of the Holy Spirit can be drowned out by the turbulent noise of the human soul. This is especially true of people that push their lives and ministries to the edge of extreme busyness. Perhaps this is the reason I Peter 3:4 tells us that a gentle and quiet spirit is precious in the sight of the Lord. The writer of Psalms 46:10 also declares, **"Be still, and know that I am God..." (KJV).**

Both of these passages seem to indicate that listening is a lost art in the human race. Furthermore, many believers today are unable to hear the still, small voice of God because most of our prayer time is spent storming the gates of heaven with an endless barrage of noisy demands. We have failed to understand that prayer is a two-way street which not only enables us to speak to God, but also lets us hear the desire of His heart.

It is important, therefore, to incorporate the "prayer of listening" into our devotional life. There are occasions when it is wise to sit down, ask nothing, and just listen. It is during those moments of blessed solitude that you will begin to sense the heart of heaven. Remember that the faintest whisper from heaven is greater in value than all the noise of religious activity.

# CHAPTER NINE

# Intuition, Perception, and Impressions

**Now when much time was spent, and when sailing was now dangerous ...Paul admonished them,**

**and said unto them, Sirs, I perceive that this voyage will be with hurt and much damage, not only of the lading and ship, but also of our lives (Acts 27:9-10 KJV).**

*I* HAD JUST FINISHED A SERIES OF MEETINGS in Fresno, California and had returned to my hotel room around 11:30 that Sunday night. I was tired and sleepy and was looking forward to a warm bed. By the time I had settled into the room, however, there was a feeling in my gut that I should check out of the hotel and make the drive back to my home in Los Angeles.

For several minutes I wrestled with this feeling of urgency and finally decided to comply. I was perplexed as to why I should leave, but I knew from past experiences that these kinds of impressions are often the voice of God speaking to me. Sleepy, but determined to obey, I loaded my suitcase into the car and checked out of my room.

After several hours of uneventful driving, I suddenly encountered a patch of thick fog which greatly impaired my vision. As I began to reduce my speed in order to navigate through the dense haze, I noticed an odd shaped object in the middle of the freeway. When I swerved to miss the object, I realized it was a person lying on the pavement. Apparently, there had been a wreck only moments earlier, and a young girl had been ejected from the bed of a truck where she had been sleeping under the camper shell.

At first I thought the child was dead and was shocked when she began to struggle to get up from the pavement. As she made it to her knees and began to crawl, I was even more horrified when a speeding vehicle came barreling out of the dense fog and ran over her legs. I immediately parked on the side of the road and bolted out of my car to where she now lay motionless. In addition to her two badly broken legs, she had a head injury and was losing blood and going into shock.

Suddenly, the Spirit of God fell on me and I understood why I was prompted to leave Fresno at such a late hour. It was now apparent that the providence of God had brought me to the aid of one of His children who was in desperate need. The situation looked grave, but I knew I was in the right place at the right time.

As I bent over the little girl and began to pray, an even greater challenge awaited me that night. In the distance, I could hear the sound of a large truck bearing down on me out of the fog. At that instant, I felt a supernatural boldness to stand up in front of the little girl as though I was a shield to the approaching tragedy. Jumping up and down, I began to wave my arms and yell, "No!" at the top of my voice. As the truck emerged out of the dense haze, the driver saw me just in time to lock-up his brakes and skid to a screeching halt several yards from me and the girl. The eighteen-wheeler was now jackknifed in the middle of the road as a barrier, blocking any threat of oncoming traffic.

Now that the immediate danger had passed, I turned my attention back to the little girl who was drifting in and out of consciousness. At that time, her mother who had also been ejected from their vehicle, crawled over and began to beg me to help her daughter. Again, the Spirit of God fell on me, and I began to rebuke the spirit of death and pray for her healing and recovery. I told the mother I was a minister and God had led me there to care for her daughter.

> Extreme purpose in God requires extreme obedience to God.

By the time the paramedics had arrived, the girl was now in a complete state of shock. Her condition looked bad, and I was instructed to leave the scene of the accident. At that point, I gave the mother my business card and returned to my car to finish the three hour drive home. As you would expect, I prayed most of the way home for the girl's recovery.

Several weeks later, I received a letter from the mother of the little girl. She began by saying that her family was raised Catholic and did not know much about the supernatural. However, she was excited to report that in spite of a head concussion and numerous broken bones, the doctors said a miracle had taken place and her daughter was mending beautifully. The mother expressed her thankfulness, but admitted she was not sure if the letter would reach me because she thought I might have been an angel sent by God.

Obviously, I am no angel, but I am happy to say that I was God's messenger sent to a little girl whose life depended on my obedience. Since that time, I have come to realize that extreme purpose in God requires extreme obedience to God—even if His voice comes to us in the form of a slight impression or a perceptive thought.

## That Certain Feeling

Are gut feelings and perceptive thoughts a sign that God is present in our spirits? If so, what is meant by the words intuition, perception, and impressions?

Actually, the three are somewhat the same and are loosely interchangeable. Intuition is knowledge that is arrived at spontaneously, independent of reason or inquiry. Perception denotes the act of apprehending by means of the senses or the mind and involves intuitive awareness. The term impression is also similar in meaning, but different in application. It is Christian slang for the slight nudge of the Holy Spirit that believers often feel deep inside their being.

For the sake of clarity, let us say that most people receive thousands of intuitive feelings on one level or another. These intuitive impressions are often interpreted as having a gut feeling, a sixth sense, being aware, or just having that certain feeling about something. It is my observation that this phenomenon is experienced by male and female, young and old, believers and non-believers alike.

This dynamic was also in operation in the New Testament era. In Mark 2:8 and Matthew 22:18, it is said that Jesus *perceived* in His Spirit the thoughts and wicked intentions of the Pharisees. Also, when Peter was addressing Simeon the sorcerer in Acts 8:23, he *perceived* the man's soul was toxic with acts of iniquity and rebuked him for his sin. Paul likewise declared in Acts 27:10 that he *perceived* danger for those sailing with him to Rome.

> Intuitive people are not necessarily godly or demonic; they are sensitive human beings with a connection to the spirit-world.

Much like these historical examples, perceptiveness is a common occurrence in the lives of people today. In my own experience, some of the most accurate information I receive comes as a result of this dynamic. You can call it intuition, gut feeling, or spiritual awareness; but the bottom line is that I have a heightened awareness to things unknowable to me at the time. I have learned to trust the Holy Spirit's ability to amplify those small, inner nudges that come from deep within my soul. This has enabled me to perceive information such as imminent danger, hidden illnesses, secret sins, and at times the thoughts and intents of people's hearts.

## Divination or Divine?

The majority of people today acknowledge intuitive impressions with statements like, "I feel strange about that" or "I wonder where that thought came from?" In many cases, they find out later that these feelings were accurate impressions of things unknowable to them at the time. This does not mean that the person is godly or demonic; it simply means that they are sensitive human beings with a connection to the spirit world.

In contrast, there are Bible teachers who believe intuition is connected to the realm of the flesh and the devil. They often talk about the dangers of dabbling into this so-called forbidden power. They are convinced that intuition is an evil power of the soul, which should forever lay dormant and unrecognized. They teach that Adam in his original state possessed a pure form of godly intuition. But, as a result of his transgression in the Garden of Eden, the power fell out of the spiritual sphere into the soulish realm where Satan is believed to have access and influence. Due to this fallen state, the use of this latent power is off-limits to everyone except sorcerers, witches, warlocks, fortune-tellers, and other spiritualists who are somewhat sensitive to the spirit realm.

While it is true we inherited an impure form of intuition from Adam, I believe the Bible teaches that fallen men are redeemable in God. This means all things lost or perverted through the fall of Adam can also be restored to their original state through Jesus Christ. By embracing the redemptive work of Jesus, the "last

Adam," intuition can be reclaimed, sanctified, and used for the kingdom of God. The principle is relatively simple: God made it pure; Satan polluted it; Jesus redeemed it at Calvary; and believers can now possess a sanctified soul.

Of course, this reality means that our whole being must be consecrated to God. No longer can we say, "Oh, I guess that was just me," or "Where did that thought come from?" If we truly believe we are saved in our spirit, soul, and body, then we must begin to rely on our inner impressions. Additionally, we should learn to trust the slightest inner nudges of God's Spirit deep within our gut. Eventually, this awareness will lead to a high level of sensitivity which will better serve our life and ministry.

## A Growing Awareness

This is not to imply that all use of intuition is good. Actually, intuitive people such as psychics, clairvoyants, and fortune-tellers often operate in a realm of divination which is forbidden by God. The difference between the divine and the demonic, therefore, has to do with who has access to our spirit, not the fact that we are intuitive. Bear in mind that a believer's intuition is in a process of sanctified reform, whereas the unbeliever still draws from the latent power of the fallen soul—a place where dark spirits have access.

In order for us to live intuitively, we must learn to rely on our sanctified soul. There must be a recognition that heaven is waiting to speak through the subtle impressions deep within our being. The Psalmist David acknowledged this phenomenon and stated in Psalms 42:7 that **"Deep calls to deep at the sound of Your waterfalls...."** No doubt, he was speaking metaphorically about a place of spiritual communion that exists between the Spirit of God and the spirit of man.

How do we facilitate this spiritual connection? Believers must begin to practice their inner perceptiveness in everyday life. If you are slow in properly discerning what you feel intuitively, do not give up—you will eventually get it right. Keep trying over and over again and you will increase to a level of keen awareness. Remember that repetition is an excellent teacher.

# CHAPTER TEN

# Mental Pictures

**Nathanael said to Him, "How do you know me?" Jesus answered and said to him, "Before Philip called you, when you were under the fig tree, I saw you" (John 1:48).**

IN THE SUMMER OF 1997, I WAS CONDUCTING a series of meetings in Central Texas. On the last day of the conference, the pastor and I were sitting around talking about everything from hunting to mechanics. Then the subject turned to automobiles and I told him I wanted to buy a used Mercedes. To my disappointment, the pastor told me that he had sold his older Mercedes several weeks before I had come to town. "If I knew you were looking for a car," he said, "I would have sold you mine really cheap."

When I left the next day, I was sad about having missed such a good deal. However, I told myself it was a good thing the car had sold because I really did not have the money to buy a Volkswagen, much less a Mercedes. It is just a fleshly desire, I mused, not a real need.

Soon, I had forgotten the whole thing and began to prepare mentally for my next meeting in the Corpus Christi area. I was deep in thought, when out of nowhere, I had a vivid mental picture of a Mercedes, dark blue in color. Instinctively I said out loud, "The Mercedes is blue and it is mine; otherwise I wouldn't have seen the color." The whole thing seemed crazy, but I felt like the car belonged to me.

A week later when I arrived home in California, my confidence began to waver. "What was I thinking?" I told myself, "No matter what I saw, it is impossible to own a car that is already sold to someone else." Once again, I distanced myself from the idea that the mental image had any real significance and began to look at less expensive cars in my area.

> Mental pictures must be submitted to the guidance of the Holy Spirit and requires extreme discretion.

Nearly a month later, my phone rang early one morning. It was the pastor in Texas. "You won't believe what happened," he said, "The man who bought the Mercedes developed serious financial problems and had to return the car." Then he paused and said, "I feel like it is your car; and if you will fly back out here, I will give it to you free of charge."

The next week I was on an airplane bound for Texas. When I arrived at the pastor's house, I saw the automobile for the first time and was elated that it was the exact same color and model I had seen in the mental picture. That weekend I drove my new car home with an appreciation for a God who would use mental images to bless my life.

Much to my joy, however, I soon discovered that my season of blessing had just begun. Not long after receiving the Mercedes, I began to have mental pictures of money falling from heaven. Every three or four days, I would have a mental flash of hundred dollar bills falling out of the sky on top of my head. On one occasion, the image was so real that I could actually smell the scent of new money.

Within several months, I was given some of the largest donations I had ever received. People felt compelled to invest into my ministry, and on one occasion, a large sum of money was given to me by a total stranger. For the rest of the year, I was blessed with financial provision from a number of different places. Suddenly, the mental images stopped and my financial status returned to normal.

## The Image Maker

Mental pictures that come without warning or forethought are often inspired by God. These pictures are much like the images seen in the subconscious mind while dreaming, yet they occur while awake. They are clearer than dreams, but not as vivid as trances or visions, and lay somewhere between the realm of natural sight and conscious thought. This phenomenon is often referred to as "seeing with the mind's eye."

Much like when a camera's eye opens momentarily to capture a scene, the mind's eye can give us snapshots of past, present, and future images. In a split second, things can be perceived that are unknown to a person's present state of mind. These pictures can come in color or in black and white and can appear in familiar form or as abstract imagery. In some instances, they have little significance. Other times they are inspired by God. They can pertain to everyday, ordinary matters of life, or they can relate to heightened activity in the spirit world.

One of the ways people in the Bible assimilated information was through mental pictures. Although it is hard to find the exact language for this phenomenon in Scripture, I believe it was a common experience for many of our spiritual forefathers. This is understandable when you consider that I Samuel 9:9 refers to prophetic people in the Bible as "seers." In a well-known example in John 1:48: Jesus *saw* Nathanael sitting under a fig tree, long before the two were ever introduced.

I also have experienced spiritual phenomena of this nature. On several occasions, I have seen mental pictures of someone ringing my doorbell prior to the arrival of an unexpected guest. I have also had images of answering my telephone only seconds before it actually began ringing. Recently, I saw an image of a beautiful rose falling to the ground several months before my mother passed away.

At other times, I have experienced mental pictures that relate to other matters of importance in the world. This included issues of imminent danger, political and social changes, devastating weather changes, economic trends, people's sins and sicknesses, the presence of angels, and other information concerning activity in the spirit realm. Several years ago, I saw a vivid mental picture of fire and great destruction in New York City, long before the terrorists brought down the Twin Towers.

## Double Vision

Can mental images serve us in our ministry to the body of Christ?

One of the ways I minister to total strangers is through inspired, mental pictures. During times of prophetic ministry, I often see images that relate to specific problems of people in the room. Sometimes I see the face of someone I know superimposed over the person I am looking at. Usually their personal history will be similar, and in most instances their names will be the same.

In a meeting in Los Angeles, I called out a man by his first name after seeing a mental picture of my friend Donald superimposed over his face. The ministry which followed included accurate information about his past and present life that was similar in nature to that of my friend. Just recently, I was also able to identify a young man in my meeting whose middle name was Allen, because every time I looked at him, I was reminded of my son, Christopher Allen. After prophesying over him, I noticed that he looked nothing like my son.

Be forewarned that the use of mental pictures must be submitted to the guidance of the Holy Spirit and require extreme discretion. What may work in one setting may not be correct in another setting. The fact that I simply see mental pictures does not mean that I have the liberty or faith to apply them anytime I please. Nor does it mean that the inspiration of the Holy Spirit is always present to help me when I try. I have learned that if I push forward without these safeguards, the results can be undesirable. If I get the name right, I can miss it with the other specifics. Or, I can get the information right and miss the name. Worse yet, I can miss the whole thing.

In spite of this difficultly, there are times when I do feel a release from the Holy Spirit to move in this area. Nevertheless, I approach it with caution and try to discern if the images have a literal application or if they are to be interpreted symbolically. For example, if I see the image of a penny while ministering to someone, does it mean her name is Penny, or is there someone named Penny in her family? Perhaps her name is not Penny, but the penny represents a spirit of poverty in her life. Again, it is necessary to trust the Holy Spirit for a proper interpretation.

> Mental pictures are a key issue in spiritual communication.

Remember that mental pictures without the witness and creativity of the Holy Spirit are just merely mental pictures. For that reason, you should never confuse daydreaming or an over-active imagination with inspired mental pictures. It is dangerous to base spiritual ministry on mental images that do not have their origin and purpose in God.

## Get the Picture?

On a more positive note, mental pictures are a key issue in spiritual communication. Yet, how do we accommodate mental images of divine origin, and are there certain things we can do to maximize the positive effect of this phenomenon?

First, we must recognize our need for a renewed mind. According to Ephesians 4:23, we should be reformed in the spirit of our mind and clothed with the nature of Christ. The author of Colossians 3:10 also implores us to **"...put on the new man who is renewed in knowledge according to the image of Him who created him" (NKJV).** This, too, implies that we have the privilege to live and minister in the character and nature of Christ.

Another way to maintain a sanctified thought life is by conditioning our minds to think optimistically. As a tree needs the proper nutrients to produce fruit, the mind must take in wholesome information in order to produce clear, revelatory thoughts. The apostle Paul affirmed this need for positive input and declared in Philippians 4:8 that we are to think on things that are innocent, pure, and lovely. He continued to say **"...whatsoever things are of good report; if there be any virtue, and if there be any praise, think on these things" (KJV).**

Last of all, we are admonished in Philippians 2:5 to possess the same state of mind that was in Christ Jesus. Paul also indicates in I Corinthians 2:16 that we are to have this mindset of Christ in order to live and walk in the Spirit. On the other hand, if there are uncertainties about the spiritual state of your mind, it would be better to disregard mental pictures until such a time that you are confidently operating in the mind of Christ (see Romans 12:2).

# CHAPTER ELEVEN

# Physical Senses

**Surely He Himself bore our griefs and He carried our sorrows; yet we ourselves esteemed Him stricken, smitten by God, and afflicted.**

**But He was pierced through for our transgressions, He was crushed for our iniquities... (Isaiah 53:4-5).**

SINCE CHILDHOOD, I HAVE HAD TROUBLE WITH my eyesight. By the time I was in the third grade, I was diagnosed with astigmatism and prescribed eyeglasses. As the years progressed, my eyes would get better for a while, but then for no apparent reason take a turn for the worse. After growing up and entering the ministry, I often thought about the paradox of being a prophetic person with failing vision.

With the passing of time, I grew accustomed to my visual limitations and nearly forgot I had a problem. Then in 1999 the unimaginable happened. I was struck with a rare eye disease that usually results in a total loss of vision. Before the disease could progress to that stage, however, it stopped suddenly leaving me with nearly total blindness in my left eye and partial blindness in my right eye.

As you might have guessed, I was left with terrible depth perception. It became impossible to tell if an object was ten feet or thirty feet away. Several times while trying to adjust to my poor eyesight, I walked off the end of the platform while preaching. While walking at home, I have also stumbled over objects that are undetectable to my limited field of vision.

> I understand the value of asking God to help us with our lack of spiritual depth perception.

I know it sounds bizarre, but I am actually comfortable with my limited eyesight. Of course, I would love to have my eyesight restored, and I have spent a lot of time praying for complete restoration. But, until that time comes, I have learned to be at peace and let God speak to me through this physical limitation.

I have learned, for example, how important spiritual vision is to my Christian journey. I now have a better understanding of the Scripture in Proverbs 29:18 that says: **"Where there is no vision, the people perish..."** (KJV).

I am convinced that my partial blindness speaks to the issue of limited vision in the church today. I have also learned that you can have spiritual vision but lack depth perception. In other words, the fact that you have prophetic insight does not mean you have the depth perception to perceive the proper approach, distance, and timing of things to come. I have found that it is one thing to see and yet another thing to see clearly and accurately.

Furthermore, God has used my disability to instruct me about the dangerous limitations of tunnel vision. When I lost my peripheral eyesight, I found out how vulnerable one can be when there is no lateral vision. Several times while driving on the freeway, these blind spots nearly cost me my life. In one instance, while walking across an intersection, I barely escaped serious injury when a vehicle outside my field of vision nearly ran over me.

How does all this relate to the church? As a result of my visual limitation, I understand the value of asking God to help us with our lack of spiritual depth perception. In addition to seeing clearly, I want to perceive the breadth, depth, and height of the spirit world around me. I have been praying lately that the Lord would give me a panoramic view of His purpose in the earth.

## Body Language

Feelings are the voice of the human body. For that reason, God will often use the pain and suffering of personal tragedy to communicate with His people. This does not mean that the Lord initiates bad things in our lives in order to teach us spiritual things. It simply means that there are times when feelings and other physical senses are used by the Holy Spirit to convey spiritual messages and information.

In addition to my partial blindness, for example, the Lord has spoken to me through a number of other physical impairments. As previously indicated, I developed an irregular heartbeat which the Lord used to teach me about the instability of the church's heart-relationship with Christ. I have also been healed of an inner ear disorder that required tubes in both ears, after acknowledging I had a spiritual hearing problem. Just recently, while fighting off a severe attack of rheumatoid arthritis (an autoimmune disorder that causes the body's cells to attack healthy tissue), I have been able to understand the internal chaos in the body of Christ that restricts our mobility.

> The Lord often communicates through any means available.

This form of communication is found in several instances in the Bible. The Psalmist David declared in Psalms 119:67, **"Before I was afflicted I went astray: but now have I kept Thy Word" (KJV).** God likewise used an undisclosed infirmity in Paul's life in II Corinthians 12:7 to teach him about the necessity of trusting in His grace. This same apostle also encountered a season of physical blindness in Acts 9:9 that enabled him to see the magnitude of his spiritual blindness.

Am I saying God impairs our physical body so He can talk to us about our spiritual weaknesses? Of course not! I am simply saying that the Lord often communicates through any means available and will use the feelings, pains, and physical impairments of the human body. If necessary, He will use them over and over again until we finally get the message.

## I Feel Your Pain

There are also times when the things we feel are a result of stuff we pick up from outside our bodies. On several occasions, I have felt unusual tremors in my body, long before an earthquake happened. On one such occasion, I literally felt the San Francisco earthquake of 1989 several weeks before it occurred. The Lord also allowed me to smell the great rainstorms of 1993, long before they arrived.

From time to time I can also feel and smell certain diseases when I get around people who are sick. The spirit of infirmity, for instance, usually smells like an unclean hospital, and cancer often smells like rotting flesh. When I come into contact with someone with the flu or a virus, I frequently feel a sensation of dizziness and weakness. Sometimes the symptoms are momentary, other times they will linger for minutes or hours.

Throughout my life, I have used the phenomenon of interpreting physical senses when ministering to the church. When I feel a burning sensation in my fingers, it is usually an indication that the anointing for the laying on of hands is present. Other times I smell the fragrance of flowers in a room, signifying that the spirit of healing is available. It is also typical for me to feel the hurts and pains of people's sicknesses who attend my meetings. Occasionally, I will describe these pains and when the person responds for prayer, the symptoms usually leave my body.

Last year, I had quite an unusual experience of this nature which lasted for a long time. For several weeks, I would wake up in the middle of the night with strange sensations in my chest. Every time this happened, I would automatically think about an acquaintance of mine named Ken. Although I was plagued with similar heart symptoms in the past, I had never had an episode during my sleep, so I knew I should pray for my friend.

Within several weeks, Ken had a heart attack and was in need of bypass surgery. Prayer was offered up for him by family and friends and he made it through the grueling ordeal. However, the prayer battle for his life on my part did not begin at the hospital, but in my bedroom several weeks before his heart failure. Thanks to God, Ken is doing fine and has returned to his normal lifestyle.

## In Touch

Because of the unpredictable nature of our physical and emotional being, discerning the voice of God through the noisy clamor of human feelings can be tricky. It would be foolish, therefore, to lead your life by physical feelings or trust them to give you spiritual direction without the help of the Holy Spirit. If you do, you will be jerked up and down like a yo-yo on the end of a string. One day you will feel one way, the next day you will feel totally different.

In light of this dilemma, what measures must we take to translate the hidden messages of our feelings into spiritual ministry?

First, in order to assure a proper interpretation, we must learn to decode the spiritual language of the physical body. The key lies in the ability to discern between the normal pains of the body and physical senses that are influenced by the Holy Spirit. If you are in pain because of nutritional neglect, for example, or because you have abused your body, then you are probably reaping the fruit of your own ignorance. However, if these pains or feelings occur only while ministering under the anointing, you could be receiving important communication from God.

Finally, if you have strange or unexpected physical feelings every time you think about someone or come into contact with them, the Holy Spirit may be provoking you to pray for their healing. If the pain or feeling of distress goes away after acknowledging that it belongs to someone around you, this, too, is an obvious sign that God is talking to you about the problems of other people.

CHAPTER TWELVE

# Nature

**For the invisible things of him since the creation of the world are clearly seen, being perceived through the things that are made... (Romans 1:20 ASV).**

SEVERAL YEARS AGO WHILE LIVING IN Southern California, I was going through one of the hardest times of my life. I was dealing with yet another season of illness, betrayal by a loved one, depression, financial collapse, and numerous other problems that threatened my life and ministry. I was sinking into a black hole of despair and was spending my nights lying awake in inner turmoil.

During one of those times on a stormy night, the Lord decided to encourage me through a little bird who sang joyfully outside my window. Alone and surrounded by bleak darkness, he began to sing at the top of his voice as though God was directing every little chirp. As I listened to this beautiful performance, the Holy Spirit began to speak to my heart through the melodic sound of the songbird.

"If a solitary bird, who has no one to encourage him, can sing in the darkness of night," He whispered, "Then surely you can cheerfully face the problems of life with the assurance that I live within your heart. Remember, I told you in the Bible that I would never leave you nor forsake you and I have sent this bird to remind you of My love."

As you might expect, I was flooded with a thousand emotions. I was challenged, encouraged, comforted, and most of all rebuked for my lack of trust in Christ. It was the beginning of a turning point that put me on a road to recovery. Before long, my condition improved and my joy began to return.

Although I never heard the little bird again, I have learned to touch God through different aspects of nature. In the years since that night, I have seen God's splendor in the rising of the sun, and have experienced His peace in the quietness of a winter morning. I have also sensed the Lord's blessing in the rain that falls on my head and have felt His breath in the wind that blows on my face. When it comes to the awe of God, I have seen His majesty in the endless expanse of the universe and His greatness in the vast depths of the ocean.

## The Nature Connection

God is constantly speaking through His creation. In Romans 1:20, the apostle Paul declared that God's eternal power and divine nature is clearly seen through that which He has made. Paul also indicated in Colossians 2:17 that things in the natural world are but a shadow of things to come.

Much like Paul, I, too, am convinced that the Creator is eager to reveal Himself through His handiwork. Honestly, we can discover a wealth of understanding about the spirit world just by observing the traits and characteristics of the created world around us. We need to open our eyes and realize that the natural world is but a silhouette of the spiritual world.

As an example, the conception and birth of a child closely parallels the principle of spiritual birth in a believer's life. Just as a wife is impregnated through intimate contact with her husband, we as the bride of Christ have been impregnated with a new birth by the seed of the heavenly Bridegroom. Jesus clearly defined this truth when He declared in John 3:3 that we must be born again in a spiritual sense.

Fundamentally, this means that the characteristics of spiritual birthing are also similar in the conception process, formation, gestation period, and complications which accompany natural pregnancy and childbirth. Paul understood this principle and addressed his spiritual family in Galatians 4:19 saying, **"My little children, of whom I travail in birth again until Christ be formed in you"** (KJV). In the books of Ephesians, he also talked about growing up into Christ through a process of spiritual development.

In this context, it is easy to understand how the seasonal cycles of trees and their fruit are similar to the development process of spiritual growth in a believer's life. As a tree sheds its leaves and puts down roots in winter, we, too, go through spiritual winters that drive our roots deep into God's soil so we can bear fruit in the next season of our ministry. It is no surprise that Isaiah 61:3 describes the people of God as **"trees of righteousness,"** the planting of the Lord.

In other examples, the characteristics and behavioral patterns of a great eagle speaks of the incredible ability of a believer to soar in the heavens and ride above the storms of life. The lion speaks about our strength and kingship; and when we observe the temperament of sheep, we can see why David declared in Psalms 100:3 that we are the sheep of God's pasture. The author of Proverbs 6:6 also stated thousands of years ago that we are to consider the ant and learn from its industrious behavior.

## The Nature of Things

As a young man, I was unaware that God wanted to speak to me through the voice of creation. Consequently, my devotional time was spent in intense prayer and intercession. I would find a quiet solitary room, lock the windows and doors, turn off the lights, and mentally prepare myself for a spiritual standoff with God. Sitting in total darkness with my eyes tightly closed for hours at a time, I would petition God to increase my spiritual hearing and vision. I was reluctant to leave until I was sure my prayers were heard in heaven.

During one of these sessions, God spoke to my heart in a most unusual manner. He gently instructed me that prayer was much more than blind repetition. He taught me that in order to receive from heaven on a larger scale,

I must open my heart and eyes to His creation that surrounded me. "When you are finished praying," He said, "Get up, open your eyes, go outdoors, and observe and learn. Study the characteristics and habits of creation and you will see My heart."

Do not get me wrong! I am not saying we should stop praying. Everyone knows that earnest prayer is one of the most vital aspects of the Christian life. I am simply saying that we must learn the language of life and connect with God through His creation. The next chance you have, clear your mind of religious activity and open your ears and eyes to the world around you. Perhaps you will be able to see and hear from the Creator.

# CHAPTER THIRTEEN

# The Cosmos

**The heavens declare the glory of God; and the firmament sheweth his handywork.**

**Day unto day uttereth speech, and night unto night sheweth knowledge.**

**There is no speech or language, where their voice is not heard (Psalm 19:1-3 KJV).**

EARLIER IN THIS BOOK I TALKED ABOUT HOW God spoke to me in a dream using the Big Dipper in the night sky. What I did not tell you is this group of stars has always been my favorite. Since I was a child, I have been fascinated with the universe and have always felt God was trying to communicate to me through different constellations of stars. In many instances, I experienced a season of breakthrough each time I saw the Big Dipper tilted in the pouring position during the night sky.

Through the course of my life, I have also been captivated by falling stars. In the beginning of my ministry, they played a significant role in confirming God's love and affirmation to my heart. For a number of years, every time I prayed outdoors the Lord seemed to mark my petition with a visual sighting of a falling star at the end of the prayer time. I believe He was saying, "I am here and your request is granted." More often than not, the answer would come within a reasonable period of time.

Recently, the Lord also spoke to me through the orbital behavior of the planet Mars. According to astronomers, Mars passed closer to earth in August 2003, than it has in the past 60,000 years. It was so close that you could clearly see the brightness of the red planet in the eastern sky. As a result of its nearness to earth, the satellites, *Spirit* and *Opportunity,* were able to land on the surface of the planet at the beginning of 2004 and send an abundance of amazing pictures and information back to earth.

> Astronomy plays an important role in understanding the effect of the cosmos on the earth.

What did I learn from these things? In a spiritual sense, I believe heaven is coming closer to earth than ever before, and at certain times we will actually see its majestic beauty from the vantage point of earth. In Luke 21:28, Jesus described this event in a spiritual context and encouraged us to lift up our heads when we see the coming brightness of His glory in the last days.

Also, the vital communication being sent back to earth by the two satellites is, in a prophetic sense, one of the signs that the necessary link between heaven and earth today has been established. In the near future we will be given the opportunity to download spiritual communication from God that has never been seen or told before.

## Astronomy or Astrology?

In our quest to hear from heaven we must never confuse astronomy with astrology. Basic astronomy, for instance, is the science and mathematics dealing with the celestial bodies of the universe, including the positions and motions of planets, stars, comets, meteors, and interstellar matter. Astrology, on the other hand, teaches that the position of these astrological bodies at the time of a person's birth, and the movement of these bodies thereafter, reflect that person's character and destiny.

I want to make it clear that I am not promoting the practice of astrology, which entails the use of the horoscope and other false systems of ascertaining the will of God. Any attempt to forecast the future by analyzing the movements of heavenly bodies or the belief that they influence individuals and the course of human events is forbidden in Scripture.

God's contempt for astrology is clearly demonstrated through the prophet Isaiah. When the prophet rebuked the Babylonians for their idolatry in Isaiah 47:13, he taunted them to seek salvation from their astrologers, stargazers, and monthly prognosticators. Apparently, their reliance on astrology compelled them to trust their lucky stars instead of trusting the Lord for guidance.

Astronomy, on the other hand, plays an important role in understanding the effect of the cosmos on the earth and its inhabitants. It is no secret that the planets and their orbital movement are like the gears of a giant clock, which marks seasons and periods of time. The author of Genesis 1:14-16 clearly states that the stars and planets are used to divide the day from night and are for signs, seasons, days, and years.

The cosmos also serves as a prophetic timepiece, foretelling special events when certain elements of the universe are emphasized and highlighted by the Holy Spirit. In an extraordinary example in Matthew 2:2-10, three Mesopotamian wise men were informed of Christ's birth by a bright star in the night sky. Although many scholars believe it was a rare alignment of Jupiter and Saturn, others suggest it was a supernova or exploding star employed by God to guide the wise men to the infant Messiah. Whichever the case, these men were able to receive a message from God by reading heaven's cosmic clock.

In other instances in the Bible, we also see God speaking through unusual cosmic activity. It is evident in Joshua 10:13 that God communicated His favor to Israel by causing the sun and moon to stand still until they could avenge themselves of their enemies. Acts 2:19 also declares that God will forecast events of the last days by speaking through wonders in heaven above and signs on the earth below.

## Symbolic Language

In addition to God speaking through the physical nature of the cosmos, the Bible also speaks of the universe in symbolic terms.

What do I mean by symbolic language? In Malachi 4:2, the Lord is metaphorically called the **"Sun of Righteousness."** Also, in Revelation 1:16, John described the appearance of the risen Christ as the sun shining at noon day. Other examples such as Psalms 84:11 and Revelation 21:23 also speak to the metaphor of Christ as the Sun and validate His place in the spiritual universe as the center of all things.

These analogies are plausible when you consider the many similarities between the natural sun and the spiritual Son. In the same way that the physical sun produces light on earth, for example, Jesus is also the Light of heaven and earth. Also, as the sun is the center of our solar system, Jesus is the central figure in the spirit world. They both sustain life on earth, and because of their brilliance, neither one can be gazed upon with the naked eye.

The Scriptures also speak of stars in symbolic terms. In Numbers 24:17, Balaam the prophet spoke about the coming Christ as a star out of the loins of Jacob. As previously stated, three wise men in Matthew 2:2 saw His star in the eastern sky and followed it to the place of Jesus' birth. Peter also spoke metaphorically of the Son of God when he declared in II Peter 1:19 that the day star (Christ) would arise in our hearts. In another example in Revelation 1:20, the writer speaks symbolically of angels and refers to them as stars in the hand of Jesus.

The moon and its physical characteristics also speak volumes, and in my opinion is symbolic of Satan. Just as the moon is described in Genesis 1:16 as a lesser light that rules the night, Satan is declared to be the prince of darkness in Ephesians 6:12. Like Satan, the moon is also smaller than the sun and has no light of its own other than the counterfeit light reflected from the rays of the sun. In Revelation 12:1, the bride of Christ is seen clothed with the sun and standing with the moon under her feet.

## Out of This World

What does all this mean? Could the sun-clad image of the woman standing on the moon, in the book of Revelation, be a prophetic sign that principalities and powers are under our feet? Could the recent eruptions of sunspots, increased solar activity, and other strange happenings discussed earlier, indicate heightened activity in the spirit world?

In all likelihood, God is speaking through both the physical and symbolic elements of His creation today. In specific terms, Jesus declared in Mark 13:8 that the beginning of turbulent times on the earth would be marked by an increase of earthquakes in various places. The author of Acts 2:19-20 also paints a picture of cosmic chaos in the last days stating, **"And I will grant wonders in the sky above and signs on the earth below, blood, and fire, and vapor of smoke. The sun will be turned into darkness and the moon into blood..."**

In light of these biblical predictions, we should be sensitive to any unusual changes in cosmic activity and ask God to reveal their meaning to us. Like the sons of Issachar in I Chronicles 12:32, we should seek for understanding the times and seasons in which we live.

# CHAPTER FOURTEEN

# People and Prophecy

**For no prophecy was ever made by an act of human will, but men moved by the Holy Spirit spoke from God (II Peter 1:21).**

ONE OF THE FONDEST MEMORIES OF GOD'S intervention in my life came as a result of an inspired message given to me by an old prophet named Robert Mitchell. Before I met this prophet, I was in total confusion about the direction of my life. I had a young family, no money, a call to ministry, and a great desire to attend Bible school.

A friend who knew this dear man of God insisted that we drive to his little cottage in rural Arkansas in order to receive a prophetic word. I was reluctant at first, but eventually agreed to make the trip. When we arrived, the prophet (nearly one hundred years old) greeted us at the door with a smile worthy of an angel. He graciously asked us into his house and arranged two chairs for us to sit on. What followed drastically changed the course of my life.

Before I was comfortable in my chair, this wonderful old man began to speak prophetically to me. He said, "I see a young man with a family. He has no finances. He is called to ministry and has been praying about going to Bible school."

He then leaned forward and looked deep into my eyes as if he knew everything else about my life. "Son, it's not God's will for you to go to Bible school. It is true you are called for ministry, but God wants to personally train you. What He has planned for you cannot be learned in a classroom. Soon God will open a door of ministry, and you will see His financial provision. So stand still and see the salvation of the Lord."

With a twinkle in his eye he continued, "Do not be disappointed. You're going to school alright, but it is going to be the school of the Holy Spirit and the school of hard knocks." Then he smiled, opened his Bible, and began to instruct me about other issues relating to my destiny. When he had finished, I knew I had seen a glimpse of God's will for my life.

> The last days are characterized by people who proclaim the advent of God's kingdom through the voice of prophecy.

Hardly two months passed before things began to fall in line with the prophetic word I had received. It became impossible for me to go to Bible school, and I was offered ministry at a church where I spent the next several years learning the true meaning of "on the job training." I encountered the difficulty of working a secular job, studying the Scriptures at night, and ministering at the church almost every weekend. When I did transition to full-time service, I was better equipped to fulfill an unusual ministry that I could not have prepared for in seminary. Thank God I listened to the word of the Lord through one of His servants instead of the conventional wisdom in my head.

## Talking for God

One of the greatest controversies in Christendom has to do with the issue of whether or not God speaks through the voice of prophecy today. Many in the church believe it is arrogant, if not impossible for men to speak for God. Others believe it is possible but unlikely, since we are living in a dispensation of time in which they believe God speaks only through the agency of Scripture.

Regardless of either view, I am convinced that God has always talked through His people and will continue until He returns to earth. In fact, He ordained scores of men and women to speak on His behalf throughout the Bible. According to II Peter 1:21, men of God spoke for the Lord as they were moved by the inspiration of the Holy Spirit. The Psalmist David confirmed this truth in II Samuel 23:2 and declared, **"The Spirit of the Lord spoke by me, and His word was on my tongue."** Zacharias also prophesied in Luke 1:70 that God has spoken through the mouth of men from the very beginning.

Other examples apply, such as the time in Genesis 20:3 when Abraham spoke the word of the Lord to

King Abimelech. Moses and Aaron were, likewise, commissioned as God's spokesmen in the book of Exodus, and both David and Samuel were well-known for their ability to articulate the heart of God. For the most part, the greater part of the Old Testament is filled with the writings of men that were deputized to speak on God's behalf.

In the New Testament era, Christ's disciples were also commissioned to speak for Him. They were instructed by the Lord in Matthew 10:7 to go into the entire world and declare **"the kingdom of heaven is at hand."** Years later, they wrote about the issue of the end times and indicated that it was a prophetic word for all to declare. In fact, Peter described the last days in Acts 2:17 as a time when our sons and daughters will proclaim the advent of God's kingdom through the voice of prophecy.

## The Gift

What is prophecy? The essence of the words "prophecy and prophesy" in the Greek language means to declare, to announce, to predict, to foretell, or to speak under inspiration. In basic terms, prophecy is God speaking through man. It is simply the authoritative announcement of God's will to man and is substantiated over four hundred times in the Old Testament where men of God declared, **"Thus says the Lord."**

The New Testament is also filled with extraordinary examples of prophecy in action. The apostle Paul instructs us in I Corinthians 14:1 to **"desire spiritual gifts,"** especially the gift of prophecy. Apparently, he understood the value of this gift and clarified its use throughout the remaining verses of chapter fourteen. He began by identifying prophecy as the primary means to encourage the people of God. This is partly due to the fact that the spiritual DNA of the prophetic consists of edification, exhortation, and comfort.

In I Corinthians 14:31, Paul also addressed the issue of who can prophesy by indicating that the voice of prophecy belongs to anyone who has a heart to build up the people of God. According to this thesis, the issue of who can prophesy is not necessarily determined by our spiritual maturity or ministry status, but by our availability and accessibility. According to Exodus 4:14, Aaron became God's spokesman, not because he was tremendously gifted, but because he was available.

Like many ordinary men in the Bible, we, too, must accept the humbling reality that God has chosen to express Himself through the frailty of mankind. The qualifying factor for that expression does not come from our performance, but from our friendship with God. Of course, prophecy is vented through the uniqueness of a person's character, voice, and language. Even so, the inspiration to prophesy comes from God and is birthed out of intimacy with Him. The bottom line is: Friends tell friends secrets.

## Inspiration or Opinion?

In spite of the importance of prophetic ministry today, we must never value prophecy above the Scriptures. The Bible is God's definitive voice and best reveals His intent for mankind today. This means prophecy should never contradict the Scriptures, nor should it stand apart from the witness of Scriptures.

Therefore, if someone gives you a message in the name of God that is crosscurrent to the principles found in the Bible, you are under no obligation to receive their word. It is not only your right to judge prophecy, but according to I Corinthians 14:29, it is your God-given duty. Paul clearly states in I Corinthians 2:15 that a spiritual man discerns all things that pertain to his life. This includes everything from slight impressions to prophetic words given by high level prophets.

> Prophecy should never contradict the Scriptures, nor should it stand apart from the witness of Scriptures.

Several years ago, I received a prophetic word from an internationally known prophet who has a reputation for accuracy. Yet, because his word was different than what God had previously revealed to me through the Scriptures, I had to put it on a shelf where it remains to this very day. I greatly respect the man's ministry and have received other prophetic words from him that have been amazingly precise. In this particular instance, however, I was forced to make the distinction between inspiration and opinion.

Does this mean I am to disrespect prophetic ministry because of one negative experience? Absolutely not! I have learned that an honest mistake made by a prophetic person does not make him a false prophet any more than a wrong diagnosis by a physician makes him a false doctor. Certainly, I must guard against such mistakes, but it would be foolish to refuse further help just because of human mistakes.

When all is said and done, I still receive guidance and comfort from the prophetic word spoken through the mouths of people today. In one instance, I was freed from several years of mental anguish by the words of a friend who said the Lord instructed him to tell me, "God does not hate your guts." He did not know that a voice had been telling me for over a year that God was displeased with me and hated my guts. When I heard the true word of the Lord through the mouth of my friend, the other voice left immediately and has never returned.

## Highlights

Now for some highlights that will serve us in the days ahead. As I have abundantly stated, God has chosen to speak through mouths of clay. He uses extraordinary people, ordinary people, educated people, uneducated people, young people, and old people. Actually, the Lord seemed to take special delight in the Old Testament by using children such as Samuel, David, and Joseph to speak His word. He also used Anna, an eighty-four year old widow, to prophesy over the infant Christ in Luke 2:36-38.

Next, it is important to the welfare of a believer to value the gift of prophecy. It is written in II Chronicles 20:20, **"believe His prophets, and you shall prosper" (NKJV).** Paul also tells us in I Thessalonians 5:20 that we should not despise the voice of prophecy or those through whom it is spoken. In several instances in the

Old Testament, Israel lost her way because they were indifferent to the word of the Lord, spoken through prophetic people.

Finally, every word from God has the potential to rout our enemies. When our destiny is confirmed by prophetic utterance, it has the potential to ward off any evil weapon that Satan has formed to destroy our future. It is clear in I Timothy 1:18 that we can wage a good warfare according to the prophecy that has been spoken over us.

CHAPTER FIFTEEN

# The Secular World

**...the Lord stirred up the spirit of Cyrus king of Persia, so that he made a proclamation throughout all his kingdom, and also put it in writing... (Ezra 1:1).**

*I*N THE EARLY YEARS OF MY MINISTRY, I WAS besieged with a number of serious issues. Primarily, I was struggling with rejection as a result of being dismissed as associate pastor from the church I was serving. I felt betrayed and had bottomed out in self-pity. No matter how long I prayed, I could not shake the feeling of failure that was dragging my soul down to a pit of despair.

After weeks of total frustration, I turned on the television one evening hoping to escape my torment. As I casually flipped through the channels, my attention was drawn to a talk show which interviewed celebrities. That evening a successful actress was talking about her climb to the top of her profession. She talked about all the problems she had encountered and the many times she was devastated through heartbreak and failure. Then as if she knew someone needed encouragement, she pointed her finger into the camera and said in a loud voice, "I CAN TELL YOU THE SECRET OF SUCCESS! DO NOT GIVE UP! KEEP ON TRYING, AND YOU WILL EVENTUALLY SUCCEED."

Although this lady was not a Christian, her words penetrated the wall of discouragement that had imprisoned my heart. In an instant my hope returned, and I felt as though I had the capacity to try again. From that moment forward, I began to pull out of my nosedive of despair and threw myself back into the work of the ministry. I was thankful that God would go to such extreme measures that He would use a secular talk show to encourage my heart. The vessel was unsuspecting, but the message was from a God who controls the thoughts of kings and paupers.

Several years later, a similar incident happened once again. While listening to a secular love song on the radio, the Holy Spirit overwhelmed me with God's love and affection. For days I could feel the closeness of the Lord in my heart and wept every time I remembered the words of the song. I was reluctant to tell anybody about my experience, for fear of criticism from a politically correct spirit.

## Secular Voices

God has never been limited to conventional means of communication. He is unpredictably diverse in the way He expresses Himself and will use any means available to get His message across. As stated in

Proverbs 21:1, **"The king's heart is like channels of water in the hand of the Lord; He turns it wherever He wishes."**

This truth is clearly seen in several instances throughout the Bible. In II Chronicles 36:23, the Lord stirred up the spirit of Cyrus, the heathen king of Persia, so that he made a righteous proclamation throughout the land. He declared, **"Thus says Cyrus king of Persia, 'The Lord, the God of heaven, has given me all the kingdoms of the earth, and He has appointed me to build Him a house in Jerusalem....'"** It is later recorded in the book of Ezra that the children of Israel did rebuild the house of God according to the word of this non-religious king.

> God has never been limited to conventional means of communication.

Another good example of God communicating through secular means is recorded in Genesis 41. The Lord troubled the heart of King Pharaoh and spoke to him three times in a dream about the coming drought on the land of Egypt. Although the magicians and wise men of Egypt were incapable of understanding the matter, Joseph was summoned from prison to give a proper interpretation of the dream. As a result, he and his father's house were spared from starvation during a time of great famine.

In less dramatic fashion, God used Rahab the harlot in Joshua 2:1 to protect two spies sent into the city of Jericho. She hid them on the roof of her house and instructed them to lay low until after nightfall. In verse sixteen, she also gave them wise counsel and instructed them to go to the hill country and hide there three days before returning to their camp. As a result, the lives of the two spies were saved, and Rahab and her family were spared when Israel later invaded the city.

God also used the cursing of Shimei in II Samuel 16:10 to test the mettle of King David's character. The angry man followed David and his servants, shouting and cursing at them. When David's men wanted to silence Shimei, the king saw an opportunity for spiritual testing and recognized Shimei as God's instrument to humble him. In verse eleven he said, **"...Let him alone and let him curse, for the Lord has told him."** Apparently, David was open to reproof from God, even if it came through the harsh words of his enemy.

## Unusual Tactics

Never underestimate the willingness of God to speak in unusual ways, especially through authority figures. Romans 13:1 proclaims, **"Every person is to be in subjection to the governing authorities: For there is no authority except from God, and those which exist are established by God."** This means we are to respect those in authority in the secular world and trust that God can use them to speak to us when necessary.

Over the years, God has spoken to me through school teachers, police officers, lawyers, doctors, and other secular means. On one occasion, while speeding to make a ministry appointment, I was stopped and severely rebuked by a police officer. After giving me a hefty ticket, he instructed me that my hurriedness was an act of irresponsibility and advised me to slow down in the future.

To say the least, I was not happy with what had transpired and was fighting a feeling of resentment. By the end of the day, however, I knew deep down in my heart that the rebuke was God-sent and that it had a two-fold meaning. In addition to being reprimanded for speeding, God was warning me about my reckless ministry schedule and was telling me to slow down. Heeding this word probably saved me from injury to myself and others around me.

I have also received God's instruction through other extraordinary means. I have discovered the wisdom of God in secular movies and have heard His voice in secular songs. The Lord has also spoken to me through historical and fictional writings, billboards on the freeway, quips and quotes in magazines, and other unusual methods. Just last year, I began to experience a new season of breakthrough shortly after hearing the words of an old secular song playing in my head. For days, the chorus rolled over and over in my mind, "Try to run, try to hide? No! Break on through to the other side."

## Creativity or Religious Spirit?

Diversity is the essence of God's nature. To some extent this means that we are made in His image for the purpose of experiencing His creativity.

Even so, there are two things that limit a believer from experiencing creative expression on this level. They are complacency and a religious spirit. Both are toxic to the issue of creativity and will keep us from moving forward in the Spirit. Actually, the definition of complacency implies a feeling of security and self-satisfaction that makes one reluctant to venture out of the familiar; whereas, the spirit of religion is defined by a striking absence of creativity.

Why is this issue so important in a believer's life? First, when a person has experienced the creativity of God, they are no longer satisfied with mere mediocrity. After tasting the freedom of spiritual creativity, you can never return to the barrenness of dead religion. To do so would discourage your heart and stifle your spiritual growth.

Next, it is possible to jeopardize our moment of visitation when we stubbornly stick to the familiar. Most likely, Moses understood this truth and turned aside from his familiar path in Exodus 3:3 to see why a bush in the desert was burning, but not consumed. As a result of his curiosity and the courage to step outside of the familiar, he encountered a visitation that forever changed the course of history.

Finally, spiritual creativity is one of the most threatening weapons against the powers of darkness. I am convinced that as long as we stick to religious ritual, the enemy can calculate our every move. It is in our best interest, therefore, to embrace acts of creativity that will keep him off balance. Satan is an expert on religious protocol and is confused when Christians experience true spirituality outside the loop of predictable religion.

# CHAPTER SIXTEEN

# Coincidence and Circumstance

**And we know that God causes all things to work together for good to those who love God, to those who are the called according to his purpose (Romans 8:28).**

AT THE AGE OF NINETEEN, I WAS RUNNING FROM my Christian heritage and had decided to become a musician instead of a minister. I was attending a vocational school in my hometown and playing guitar in a rock band on the weekends. I had told myself that one day when I was older, I would give my heart back to God and fulfill the calling that had been on my life since childhood. For the time being, I just wanted to finish the drafting class and lose myself in my music.

For several years, I went down this road of denial until a strange series of coincidences began to get my attention. One night, while walking home from the Vo-Tech School, I noticed that a particular streetlight went out the instant I passed under the light. At the time, I did not think much about it and figured it was just a mere coincidence. There had to be a logical explanation and I was determined not to be spooked by the incident.

To my amazement, however, the same thing happened the following night at the exact same time and place. Strangely, the streetlight went out every time I passed under it for nearly a week. Bewildered by these odd events, I consulted my father who was a minister. After telling him about the situation, he said, "Son, God has been trying to talk to you for a long time, but you won't pay attention. You won't listen to me or to His Word. Now the Lord is using this to tell you that if you do not change your life, He's going to put out your light."

> Circumstances and coincidences often work together in shaping our destiny.

It was a hard word, but I knew Dad was right. I knew this was not just a series of weird coincidences, but the voice of God speaking through divine circumstance. That day I promised the Lord I would go back to church the following weekend. "If God still wants me," I thought, "I might even give my heart back to Him."

As the week went by, however, I began to lose my sense of conviction. That Saturday night, I played my guitar in a local nightclub until three in the morning and when I got home, I was so tired that I decided to sleep instead of keeping my vow to go to church. I was out like a light. Then around seven o'clock that Sunday night, I was awakened by the loudest claps of thunder I had ever heard. For the next hour, I lay in bed feeling like a disobedient child, chastised by the bolts of lightning and loud thunder. Again, I was certain this was no coincidence, but the rumblings of God's voice speaking through the storm.

As you might expect, I went to church the next Sunday night. My plan was to show up late and hide in the back of the building. Yet, when I arrived, the only seat available was a center chair on the front row. I had no choice but to sit right between the pastors and other leaders. Once again, I knew this was more than a coincidence and that as a result of a divine circumstance, God had me where He wanted me. He seemed to be saying that my place in life was on the front row, sitting with leadership.

Now under a strong conviction, I went up at the end of the service to give my heart back to God. When I reached the front of the church, I threw myself on the altar and began to beg God to forgive me and use me any way He saw fit. After a long period of soul-searching and deep repentance, I arose from my knees feeling like a new man. For the first time in my life, my heart was filled with a strange sense of destiny.

The following morning, I was so overjoyed that I went fishing, just so I could sit in solitude and meditate on the events that had transpired. For the third time, I encountered the voice of God through a circumstance— within an hour I had caught so many fish, I could not drag them up the hill to my car. Since I rarely ever caught fish in this spot, I knew this, too, was no coincidence. God was speaking through divine providence, saying that He was giving me an anointing for abundance and that my net would always be full.

## Coincidence or Divine Providence?

What are coincidences and circumstances? *Webster's Dictionary* defines a coincidence as a "striking occurrence by mere chance of two or more events at one time." Circumstance is defined as "a condition or attribute that accompanies, determines, or modifies a fact or event."

In the physical world, circumstances and coincidences are common happenings of everyday life. The two often work together in shaping our destiny. It is the circumstances of life that push us toward unknown destinations, and coincidences that make us scratch our head along the way.

As depicted in the previous story, these two dynamics of life are not always random events, but are often orchestrated by God. For example, when Balaam's donkey suddenly turned from its path, it was not a mere circumstance, but the donkey responding to an unseen angel standing in the middle of the road. What seemed like happenstance to Balaam was the providence of God speaking through the stubbornness of a donkey, warning the prophet of his folly (see Numbers 22:22-31).

Jonathan, the son of King Saul, also demonstrated that God rules in the realm of circumstance and coincidence. In I Samuel 14:11, he tested this theory in battle by committing the deciding factor for victory to the hands of "chance." Jonathan's plan was to reveal himself to a garrison of Philistine warriors, and if by "chance" they said: "Stay where you are and we will come to you" it would be a sign to retreat. But, if the Philistines said,

"Come to us," Jonathan would take this "coincidence" as the voice of God summoning him to storm their camp. Consequently, the enemy signaled Jonathan to come over to them, and he and his armor bearer arose in faith and slaughtered twenty enemy soldiers.

The same principle was also put to the test in Gideon's life. In Judges 6:37, the warrior submitted the question of God's will to what seemed to be mere chance. His plan was to put a fleece of wool on the ground overnight and if there was dew on the fleece the next morning and nothing on the ground, he believed God was going to deliver Israel from their enemies. When this strange phenomenon occurred twice, Gideon and his men of war boldly pursued the enemy.

## Practical Wisdom

As seen in the previous examples, what looks like chance is frequently the voice of God speaking in the natural world of circumstance. In view of this phenomenon, we must have faith to perceive God behind the door of coincidence and hear His voice in the smallest circumstance. When these two dynamics are at play in a believer's life, the potential for success is unlimited.

On the other hand, circumstances and coincidences should never replace the leading of the Spirit. There is a thin line between physical circumstances and divine intervention, which is critical to the issue of guidance. This means we must learn to distinguish between the ordinary occurrences of life and God-influenced circumstances. This requires a high-level of sensitivity to the Holy Spirit and a good dose of common sense.

Occasionally, circumstances can also stand in the way of God's will. The fact that things happen in life does not give us an absolute guarantee that our destiny is arbitrarily decided by circumstances. There are times when negative circumstances must be properly discerned and confronted. Such was the case in Acts 27, when Paul would not allow the negative circumstances that left him shipwrecked and marooned on a remote island turn him aside from the path of his destiny.

Like Paul, we, too, must recognize the delicate balance between the normal everyday circumstances of life and that which is influenced by God or the devil. The trick is to embrace the circumstances that the Holy Spirit is using to communicate God's will and resist the circumstances the enemy is using to detour us from God's will. Also, there are certain times when coincidences and circumstances cannot be assigned to either God or the devil, and in my opinion must remain as natural occurrences in life.

# CHAPTER SEVENTEEN

# The
# Scriptures

**For the word of God is living, and active and sharper than any two-edged sword, and piercing as far as to the division of soul and spirit, of both joints and marrow, and able to judge the thoughts and intentions of the heart (Hebrews 4:12).**

WHEN I FIRST DEDICATED MY LIFE TO CHRIST, I was eager to hear everything God was saying to my heart. I went from meeting to meeting hoping that someone would call me forward and give me a prophetic word. In one particular meeting, I approached an evangelist and asked him to pray and see if the Holy Spirit would speak to him about the will of God for my life. Annoyed by my request, he put his hands firmly on my shoulders and said, "You need to get into the Bible. If you knew the Word of God, you wouldn't be asking me about His will for your life. Obviously, you haven't learned that His Word is His will."

This was not the response I was looking for, and I was a little angry to be treated in a manner that I felt was disrespectful. Still, as time passed, I could not get away from the admonition of the evangelist. Day after day my head tried to reject his instruction, but my heart told me that the Bible was God's voice and will. I finally conceded and buried myself in reading and meditation of the Scriptures. Little did I know that it would be my connection to God's voice and the yardstick by which I would measure all spiritual experiences that followed.

> God is unpredictably diverse in the way He expresses Himself.

After a long season of extensive Bible study, the inevitable began to happen. While reading about the ministry of Aaron the High Priest in the book of Exodus, the Scriptures seemed to leap off the page right into my heart. Every word was tailor-made for me and went deep into my spirit. The more I read Exodus 28 and 29, the more I was able to see the will of God for my life and ministry.

From that time forward, I began to receive instruction through various other Scriptures and stories in the Bible. When I encountered a season of rejection, for example, the Lord encouraged me through the life of Joseph. Later, when I came into a season of favor and prosperity, He used the story of Abraham to guide my footsteps. On other occasions, the Lord has instructed me through the Psalms of David, the Proverbs, the Song of Solomon, and even the book of Ecclesiastes.

In recent years, God has also spoken to my life through a number of other Bible narratives, as well as through the writings of the Old Testament prophets and the apostles in the New Testament. I have benefited from the failures and successes of men like Isaiah, David, Solomon, Peter, Paul, and other great patriarchs. I have come to understand that every word in the Bible is laden with wisdom when highlighted to your heart by the Holy Spirit.

## The Living Word

I am often asked if the Scriptures provide us with a level of communication that is equivalent to a personal word from God.

For a definitive answer to this question, one must understand several important truths. First, the Bible is the premier will and voice of God. For this reason, I decided to address the subject of hearing God's voice through the Bible in the last part of this book. I made this decision, not because it is less important, but because I wanted to end with the most reliable and authoritative voice of God.

Next, John 1:1 establishes the origin of God's Word saying, **"In the beginning was the Word, and the Word was with God, and the Word was God."** John continued this thought in verse 14 saying, **"And the Word became flesh, and dwelt among us, and we saw His glory, the glory as of the only begotten of the Father, full of grace and truth."** This same apostle also wrote in Revelation 19:13 that he saw a vision of the resurrected Christ, and His name was called **"The Word of God."**

In light of these Scriptures, it is clear that the cornerstone of Christianity rests on the fundamental doctrine of oneness between Christ and the written Word. It would be an act of heresy, therefore, to separate the voice and will of Jesus from Scripture, either in doctrine, theology, or practice. Jesus clearly understood the connection between Himself and the Word and stated in John 5:39 that the Scriptures are **"...those that testify about Me."**

All of these things lead to the conclusion that the voice of Christ and His Word are one and the same. He is the essence of both the Logos (written word) and the Rhema (spoken word). He *was* the Word of God sent from heaven in human form over two thousand years ago, and through the inspiration of the Holy Spirit, He *is* the Living Word today. Consequently, to hear the voice of the Spirit, you have only to know and understand the Word of God; for the two bear witness to each other.

## The Voice of the Scriptures

The will of the Lord for our lives is often confirmed through the voice of Scripture. Knowing this to be true, I have engaged in a number of spiritual disciplines which have increased my receptivity to God's voice. As stated, in the early years of my ministry, I buried myself in volumes of Scripture and studied until the early hours of the morning so I could clear my head of confusion and hear from heaven. I also committed Scripture to memory in order to reprogram my negative way of thinking. Eventually my mind went through a renewing process and God began to use the Scriptures to speak to me concerning my ministry and other aspects of life.

I also found that a steady diet of Bible reading nourished my soul and provided me with a communication link to heaven. Jesus affirmed this truth in Matthew 4:4 saying, **"Man shall not live by bread alone, but on every word that proceeds out of the mouth of God."** To accommodate this spiritual dynamic, I occasionally play recordings of the Bible in my house during the day and while asleep at night. I have found it is easy to get the Scripture into my mind and spirit when I hear it in audible form.

Equally important, I pray through the Bible out loud when I need to press God for an urgent response. I have come to understand that prayers launched from the foundation of God's Word cannot return void, but will evoke a swift response from heaven. I have also discovered that verbal confession of Scripture is a way of initiating a two-way conversation with the Spirit of God. The Psalmist David said in Psalms 86:7, **"I will call upon thee: for thou wilt answer me" (KJV).**

Psalms 119:105 also records that the Word of the Lord is a lamp unto our feet and a light unto our path. "A lamp to our feet" speaks to the issue of direction in our everyday walk; whereas a "light to our path" indicates an ongoing work of illumination that directs our future steps. Consequently, any Scripture that is read, prayed, memorized, or quickened to your heart has the potential to lead you down the path of your God-given destiny.

Also, sudden flashes of Scriptures in your mind and Bible stories that linger in your memory can provide the spark which ignites the illumination of the Holy Spirit in your life. Remember that the Bible is the ultimate revelation of God's voice and will for mankind.

# CHAPTER EIGHTEEN

# The
# Last Word

**And they heard the voice of the Lord God
walking in the garden in the cool of the day:
and Adam and his wife hid themselves from
the presence of the Lord God amongst the
trees of the garden (Genesis 3:8 KJV).**

*H*OW DOES ONE END A BOOK ON HEARING THE
voice of God? It seems we must go full circle back
to the Garden of Eden and explore the beginning of our
future. It was there that God first communicated with
our ancestors, Adam and Eve.

The implication in Genesis 3:8 is that Adam and Eve
fellowshiped on a daily basis with God's presence that
stirred in the wind of Eden. The problem, however, was
that there were two voices and two trees in the Garden.
In addition to the sound of God's presence, there was
the sound of the serpent (which was Satan in physical
form). What's more, there was a Tree of Life of which
God had given Adam and Eve permission to eat and a
Tree of Knowledge which was forbidden.

Knowing this, the serpent verbally seduced Eve, who without hesitation convinced Adam to disobey God and eat the fruit of the forbidden tree. Because of this disobedience, their eyes were opened to their nakedness and they hid themselves among the foliage of the garden from the presence of the Lord. When God called out to Adam for an explanation he replied, **"I heard thy voice in the garden, and I was afraid, because I was naked; and I hid myself" (Genesis 3:10 KJV).**

As a result of their sin, a curse was evoked on Adam and Eve; and as an act of mercy, God clothed them with garments of skin and banished them from the Garden. The Lord was concerned that man, now knowing good and evil, would eat from the Tree of Life and live forever in a fallen state. To prevent this, He placed cherubim and a flaming sword at the east entrance of the Garden to guard the way to the Tree of Life.

## The Other Voice

How does all this speak to the issue of hearing the voice of the Lord?

Primarily, Adam and Eve were made for communion with God. This was undoubtedly an insult to Satan who once served as chief communicator in heaven, long before his fall from grace. According to Isaiah 14:12, he was not only cut off from the throne of God, but also cast out of the heavens onto the earth. Because this fallen angel had lost his influence in heaven, his intention was to sabotage the communication lines between God and man and introduce his own diabolical voice into creation.

The plan was simple but effective. As Adam and Eve walked with God in the Garden, the "evil one" lurked in the shadows, calculating his approach. When the time was right he ambushed Eve and accomplished the unthinkable. Through cunning words the serpent appealed to the carnal ear of Eve with the phrase, "Has God really spoken?" Eve then convinced Adam to disregard God's voice, and both of them entered into a demonic covenant that would bring devastation to countless generations.

It seemed that Satan had accomplished his objective. In the past, he was unable to directly harm God; but now he had found a way to hurt the heart of the Creator by defiling the soul of those made after God's image. Satan's evil seed would now take root in the soul of man and fallen humanity would bear the profile of evil, as opposed to the image of the godly. So great was this transference of evil that several millenniums later, Jesus recognized this seed of enmity in a group of Pharisees and declared in John 8:44, **"You are of your father the devil."**

## Fallen State

In regard to the fallen state of humanity, there is a statement in Romans 5:12 that is absolutely profound. Paul writes: **"Wherefore, as by one man sin entered into the world, and death by sin; and so death passed upon all men, for that all have sinned" (KJV).**

What does the apostle mean by this Scripture? First, I believe man is a threefold being made up of spirit, soul, and body. In the case of Adam, the order of these things was vital to his relationship with God. He was in his created form, a spirit-man with a soul that lived in a body. In other words, his spirit was predominate and ruled over his soul and body. This accounted for the fact that Adam could clearly hear the supernatural sound of God's voice in the Garden of Eden.

As indicated, Adam and Eve reversed the order of creation when they sinned against the Creator. Due to the Fall, an inversion of sorts took place. No longer was Adam a spirit-being with a soul, but he was now a soul-man with a spirit. When he transgressed and was put out of the Garden, the spiritual side of his being fell into the realm of his soul where it lay dormant. His spirit was now subservient to his soul. In all probability, the farther he walked away from Eden, the fainter God's voice became in his spirit.

> Like Adam and Eve, we live with two voices struggling for supremacy of our hearts.

The sad truth is that Adam's fallen state greatly affected the core of humanity. According to the apostle Paul, his sin was passed down from generation to generation, separating mankind from the presence of God. The apostle declared in Romans 5:18 that Adam's offense brought judgment on us all. Because of this offense, generations of men fell short of God's glory and learned to exist outside the walls of spiritual paradise.

The same is true today. Because of our identification with Adam, we are victims of his inverted state of being. Like Adam and Eve, many of us live with two voices struggling for supremacy of our hearts. With the passing of every day, the voice of the Lord grows fainter and fainter, while the voice of the serpent continues to dispute whether God has spoken at all. The more we indulge ourselves in the fallen nature of Adam, the more we are prone to hide from the presence of God.

## Reverse the Curse

What is the answer? Can we really return to the place of spiritual communion with God that Adam and Eve possessed in the Garden? If so, what role do the cherubim and flaming sword play in this journey?

First, I believe it is possible to recapture our created spiritual state. The Bible tells us that God has given mankind yet another chance to return to the Garden and partake of the Tree of Life. However, this garden is not organic, nor is the tree literal. The New Testament indicates that paradise is a spiritual place where Jesus, the second Adam, has His existence and being. For all intents and purposes, He is the Living Tree of eternal life that God transplanted into the soil of humanity nearly two thousand years ago. It is written in 1 Corinthians 15:45, **"...the first man Adam was made a living soul; the last Adam** (Jesus) **was made a quickening spirit" (KJV).**

In a striking example in John 3:15, the author strengthens this truth saying: **"That whosoever believeth in him should not perish, but have eternal life (KJV)."** It is likewise stated in John 17:3, **"And this is life eternal, that they might know thee the only true God, and Jesus Christ, whom thou hast sent" (KJV).** The Lord also spoke in metaphoric terms about His association with the Tree of Life and severely offended the Pharisees when He stated in John 6:53, **"...unless**

**you eat the flesh of the Son of Man and drink His blood, you have no life in yourselves."**

In spite of the extreme nature of these Scriptures, the Holy Spirit was simply saying that the path back to the Tree of Life in Eden was pioneered by Jesus of Nazareth. This last Adam voluntarily walked the long road to Calvary's hill knowing that He was about to face the flaming sword of God. Historically speaking, He was nailed to a cross, on the east side of Jerusalem and lifted up between heaven and earth, toward the gate of paradise. At the ninth hour of the day, He finally passed through the flaming sword of judgment, bearing the curse of humanity in His own body. Afterwards, He was ushered into the presence of God by the angelic guardians of paradise.

The apostle Paul put it into perspective when he wrote in I Corinthians 15:22, **"For as in Adam all die, so also in Christ all will be made alive."** Therefore, to reverse the curse of spiritual deafness and return to the sound of God's voice, we, too, must make the journey back to the beginning of our future. This cannot be done through good works or religious performance, but is accomplished through identification with Jesus, the last Adam.

## Conclusion

Why is this connection to the last Adam so critical to our spiritual journey? According to John 6:51 and 14:6, Jesus is the way, the truth, the living word, and the voice of God; and those who hear and believe His voice will find eternal life. The Lord further declared in Revelation 3:20, **"Behold, I stand at the door, and**

**knock: if any man hear my voice, and open the door, I will come in to him, and sup with him, and he with me" (KJV).**

It is also stated in John 5:25 that the hour will come when the dead will hear the voice of Jesus and live. No doubt this Scripture makes reference to the last days and those who will rise from their grave to resurrection life at the return of Christ. Even so, I believe there is a secondary meaning that speaks to the theme of this book. To put it bluntly, we are walking, dead men when we cling to the fallen attributes of the Adamic nature. In Adam we cannot touch, hear, or commune with God. The apostle Paul makes it clear in I Corinthians 2:14 that the natural man does not receive the things of the Spirit of God—neither can he know them because they are spiritually discerned.

In order to live in Christ at the present time, our only hope is to be awakened from the sleep of Adam by the sound of His voice. As described in this book, that sound comes in many different ways, and those who perceive it are uniquely diverse in the way they hear. This means there is no arbitrary method or set formula as to the issue of hearing from God. Everyone must find our their unique connection to God's voice and learn to communicate creatively. Remember that it is not about the method, but about the message.

**"He who has an ear, let him hear what the Spirit says to the churches..." (Revelation 2:11).**

THE END

# The Morning Star Journal

Each quarterly edition of *The Morning Star Journal* ® includes timely articles on subjects such as hearing from God, church life, church structure and authority, prayer, spiritual warfare, worship, and prophecy. Edited by **Rick Joyner**, with contributing editors **Jack Deere**, **Francis Frangipane**, and **Dudley Hall.** Articles are included by respected teachers and writers from both the present and the past.

## One Full Year
## Only $16.95
Item # MAG

- Shipping is included
- No other discounts apply to this service
- Prices may be subject to change without notice

Foreign subscription
Item # FMAG $24.95USD

## Call 1-800-542-0278 to subscribe!
## www.morningstarministries.org